"This book offers direct advice from experienced experts on a mosaic of topics surrounding the implementation of HR technology. It's an important collection of work for those looking to implement or expand their HCM landscape."
Karen Heatwole, Vice President, Human Capital Management Center of Excellence, SAP

"Brilliant, perceptive, and insightful—a must read for anyone implementing or supporting an SAP implementation. This book provides the tools necessary to be successful and a leader in the world of SAP HCM."
Hermes Mendez, Director, ICTS, Orange County Public Schools

"There is no other book like this on the market written by consultants who all have great experiences. This is a must read for existing clients, anyone considering implementing SAP HR, and anyone teaching SAP HR."
Dr. Lou Thompson, Professor of Enterprise Management Systems, University of Texas at Dallas

SAP Lessons Learned—Human Capital Management

SAP Experts Share Experiences to Directly Impact Your Next Initiative

By:

Scott Burton
Steven Chihos
Michael Feast
Tracey Groomes
Raaz Karimi

Saaz Karimi
Sean Mallon
LaShonda Rahming
Jan Redmond
Maxine Wood

20660 Stevens Creek Blvd., Suite 210
Cupertino, CA 95014

Copyright © 2012 by LaShonda Rahming

All rights reserved. No part of this book shall be reproduced, stored in a retrieval system, or transmitted by any means electronic, mechanical, photocopying, recording, or otherwise without written permission from the publisher.

Published by Happy About®
20660 Stevens Creek Blvd., Suite 210, Cupertino, CA 95014
http://happyabout.com

First Printing: January 2012
Paperback ISBN: 978-1-60005-217-0 (1-60005-217-7)
eBook ISBN: 978-1-60005-218-7 (1-60005-218-5)
Place of Publication: Silicon Valley, California, USA
Paperback Library of Congress Number: 2011961232

Trademarks

All terms mentioned in this book that are known to be trademarks or service marks have been appropriately capitalized. Neither Happy About®, nor any of its imprints, can attest to the accuracy of this information. Use of a term in this book should not be regarded as affecting the validity of any trademark or service mark.

Warning and Disclaimer

Every effort has been made to make this book as complete and as accurate as possible. The information provided is on an "as is" basis. The author(s), publisher, and their agents assume no responsibility for errors or omissions. Nor do they assume liability or responsibility to any person or entity with respect to any loss or damages arising from the use of information contained herein.

About Us

ALL About Collaboration is a lean, fiercely independent platform founded by LaShonda Rahming in 2010 that is dedicated to providing useful information using an open innovation platform. ALL About Collaboration has worked with each of these authors to create content that would be useful to anyone that is on an SAP Project team, on a production support team, or is looking to implement the SAP Human Capital Management module. If you have not already registered to be a part of our exciting platform, please do so at http://www.allaboutcollaboration.com and learn more about us.

The Website—An Extension of this book

This book and its website, http://www.allaboutcollaboration.com, have been designed to work together to organize and present useful information that extends the material of this book. More importantly, the website is an effective way to experience and share information among our community of readers. Here is what you will find there:

- A growing and ever-expanding list of certified and non certified third party solutions where you can add your opinion and see opinions from others.

- A Polling Center where you can share your opinions and see the opinions of others on various topics related to the SAP Solutions, Professional Services and your favorite consultants.

- An event calendar to keep you up to date with our face to face SAP Professional networking events. These events include parties at SAP events such as SAPPHIRE and ASUG, Insider conferences, local gatherings, and even an annual family friendly networking cruise.

Acknowledgments

At the end of each initiative I created a document named Lessons Learned. I have done this for most of my career and sometimes I even create a PowerPoint presentation to send to the entire team called Quips-n-Quotes, which is inspired from the Lessons Learned document. It is so important to understand what could have been done better to avoid the same mistakes. With this, I would like to say thank you to my clients, project team members, and mentees that I have worked with throughout my career. The ideas from this book come from each of you.

I would like to thank each of the authors of this book. This effort has been collaborative, as we have all worked together to make this happen. Each author is an expert in his or her own right and has contributed significantly to the SAP community.

I would also like to thank my family for their support and the ALL About Collaboration family for continued support as we are working hard to provide value to the SAP community.

Human Capital Management Authors

Scott Burton

Steven Chihos

Michael Feast

Tracey Groomes

Raaz Karimi

Saaz Karimi

Sean Mallon

LaShonda Rahming

Jan Redmond

Maxine Wood

A Message from Happy About®

Thank you for your purchase of this Happy About book. It is available online at: http://happyabout.info/saplessonslearned.php or at other online and physical bookstores.

- Please contact us for quantity discounts at sales@happyabout.info
- If you want to be informed by email of upcoming Happy About® books, please email bookupdate@happyabout.info

Happy About is interested in you if you are an author who would like to submit a non-fiction book proposal or a corporation that would like to have a book written for you. Please contact us by email at editorial@happyabout.info or phone (1-408-257-3000).

Other Happy About books available include:

- 42 Rules of Employee Engagement:
  http://www.happyabout.com/42rules/employee-engagement.php
- 42 Rules for Successful Collaboration:
  http://www.happyabout.com/42rules/successful-collaboration.php
- 42 Rules for Your New Leadership Role:
  http://www.happyabout.com/42rules/yournewleadershiprole.php
- Scrappy General Management:
  http://bit.ly/bfFS7s[1]
  Scrappy Project Management:
  http://happyabout.com/scrappyabout/project-management.php
- Climbing the Ladder of Business Intelligence:
  http://www.happyabout.com/climbing-ladder.php
- #IT OPERATIONS MANAGEMENT tweet Book01:
  http://happyabout.com/thinkaha/itoperationsmanagement.php
- #LEADERSHIPtweet Book01:
  http://www.happyabout.com/thinkaha/leadershiptweet01.php
- #PRESENTATION tweet Book01:
  http://www.happyabout.com/thinkaha/presentationtweet01.php
- #BUSINESS SAVVY PM tweet Book01:
  http://happyabout.com/thinkaha/businesssavvypmtweet01.php
- #PROJECT MANAGEMENT tweet Book01:
  http://happyabout.com/thinkaha/projectmanagementtweet01.php
- #RISK MANAGEMENT tweet Book01:
  http://happyabout.com/thinkaha/riskmanagementtweet01.php

---

1. www.happyabout.com/scrappyabout/scrappy-general-management.php

Contents

Introduction	Brutally Honest	1
Chapter 1	**Lessons Learned about Bandwidth** **By Scott Burton**	**3**
	Introduction	3
	Bandwidth	4
	Resource Training	6
	Managing Turnover	8
	Creating True Business Value	11
	Key Learnings	12
Chapter 2	**The Fixed Priced Model** **By Raaz Karimi**	**15**
	Fixed Price	15
	T&M (Time and Material)	17
	Resources	18
	Training	19
	Communication	20
Chapter 3	**The Four Quadrants of a SAP Learning Project** **By Tracey Grooms**	**23**
	Consultant Fit	25
	"Learning Life Cycle" in the Organization	26
	Continuity of Content	27
	Metrics	27
Chapter 4	**Overcoming Post-Go Live Resistance to Change** **By Steven Chihos**	**29**
	Summary	36

Chapter 5	**Lessons Learned from E-Recruiting** **By Saaz Karimi** **39**
	1. Testing: The Importance of Testing Extensively . . . . 40 2. Customization: Heavy Customization Vs. Out of the Box . . . . 41 3. Enhancement Framework . . . . 42 4. End-User Training and Change Management as Part of the Implementation Cycle . . . . 42 5. Lessons Learned as Part of the Implementation Cycle . . . . 43 6. The use of ALE when implementing E-Recruitment 44
Chapter 6	**Don't Reinvent the Wheel: Explore SAP Partner Solutions!** **By Sean Mallon** **49**
	The Value-Added Hand of an SAP Partner . . . . 50 A Client's Gap and Inept Solution . . . . 52 A Valuable Lesson . . . . 53 The Roads Less Taken . . . . 53 Conclusion 56
Chapter 7	**The Intangibles** **By Jan Redmond** **57**
Chapter 8	**Lessons Learned with SAP Benefits Administration** **By Maxine Wood** **65**
	Point One—Adjustment Reason Start Date Versus Plan Start Date in the Back Office and through ESS . . . . 65 Point Two—When to Create the Open Offer as an Adjustment Reason. 69
Chapter 9	**SAP End-User Productivity Case Study** **By LaShonda Rahming** **73**
Chapter 10	**Time Management Lessons Learned** **By Michael Feast** **85**

Appendix A	Contributors' Background	**93**
Editor	About the Editor	99
Books	Other Happy About® Books	101

Introduction

Brutally Honest

As you might guess from the name of the book, our Lessons Learned book is a look at functionality, project management, change management and even third party software solutions from very experienced consultants. We will tell you exactly what we'd tell a good friend if she/he called us and asked what we really thought. We do believe, that in a world of advertorials and user generated review websites, consumers deserve a hard-nosed advocate that can deliver the unvarnished truth. We hope to help you avoid some of the pitfalls that we have experienced with SAP customers all over the world.

If you consult for or manage SAP projects of any kind, this book is for you. If you collaborate with co-workers to solve SAP problems or create systems, devices, or SAP products, this book is for you. If becoming a leader in your industry by improving your ability to ask the right questions and document the answers is important to you, this book is for you.

This book is a comprehensive guide that outlines lessons that have been learned from many experts in the SAP Human Capital Management field. We hope you can use this book to accomplish three goals:

1. Improve your knowledge of the SAP Human Capital Management solutions
2. Help you to improve your production support plan

3. Ensure that you and your end-users have a resource to be innovative and effective long after your SAP solution has been implemented

Chapter 1

Lessons Learned about Bandwidth

By Scott Burton

Introduction

Supporting SAP HR operations can be challenging for IT and business professionals alike. Many factors contribute to the complexity of supporting SAP HR—some that are controllable and some that are not.

Human Resource business processes are always changing; they are far from being static. Keeping up with changing business requirements is a continuous challenge. Some of these changes can be planned in advance, but in many cases HR is given little advance notice for even major changes like re-organizations and acquisitions.

Additionally HR is very much a cyclical business. Annual events like payroll year-end processing, benefits open enrollment, and performance management cycles bring with them increased support workload for an operations staff already functioning at full capacity. Add to this changing regulatory and compliance dictates, and you begin to see the hectic nature of supporting SAP HR.

There is yet another side to the complexity of supporting SAP HR. The system itself is continuously changing and constantly being enhanced. Bug fixes are provided through OSS notes and enhancement packs are released periodically to deliver new functionality for standard processes. Further issues that complicate HR support operations include unrealistic expectations from the users, and their ever-changing requirements.

So where does it all start? Most companies face an uphill battle from the beginning. In most cases SAP HR is implemented by external consultants with some internal resources assigned to the project to "learn SAP" during the project phase. In the majority of cases this knowledge transfer typically never takes place. Documentation slides to the end of the project and most often times is never completed. Additionally, most implementation projects go live with outstanding open issues that often linger for months and sometimes years.

Most HR IT support organizations are measured by responsiveness, accuracy, system stability, and the business value of their work. To score well, these organizations must deal with many challenges. Key challenges typically experienced by organizations supporting SAP HR include bandwidth, resource training, managing turnover, and ultimately creating true business value. In this chapter we'll explore these top four challenges faced by organizations supporting SAP HR and ways to overcome them.

Bandwidth

Bandwidth is one of the most common challenges in supporting SAP HR. Bandwidth is usually measured in terms of the number of available resources. However, there is much more to it than that. Bandwidth is having enough resources at the right time with the right skills to keep pace with business requirements.

Consider payroll support as an example. At least one person is needed for this function because payroll requires specialized skills. Under normal circumstances, this person can provide the required 'bandwidth' needed to support payroll operations. However, normal is not always the case. Perhaps it's year-end or unanswered payroll issues that have stacked up. If there are eighty hours of payroll issues to resolve and only three days to resolve those issues, having the right resource is not enough. In this case, more resources are needed at this specific time. Again, bandwidth is having enough resources at the right time with the right skills.

Most bandwidth challenges stem from budget constraints, extended absences like vacation, FMLA, and sick time, as well a mounting issue backlog and the arrival of multiple critical business requirements arriving at the same time. Bandwidth challenges tend to show themselves even more during critical HR operations cycles like Payroll Year-end, Benefits Open Enrollment, and Performance and Compensation review periods. One thing for certain is these events will occur at some point in time during the month, the quarter, or the year.

Bandwidth limitations can have a serious impact to the organization, particularly when issues take a long time to resolve, or worse do not get resolved. Too often is the case that issues have been open for extended periods and often for more than six months. As new critical issues arise, existing issues are eventually reprioritized downward or put on hold. Lost in the mix is that these reprioritized issues still remain very important to some part of the organization but continue to be unresolved. This is when satisfaction levels begin to erode.

Another issue is quality. As bandwidth constraints lead to time constraints, certain aspects of issue resolution are side-stepped or not performed thoroughly. Unit testing and documentation are prime examples. Sometimes these time constraints lead to rushed work which produces errors. In other cases workarounds are used to save time, only to add additional cost later because the root cause of the problem is never resolved and the problem resurfaces. An example is struggling to get payroll issues resolved prior to the weekly deadlines. The shortcut may be to lock employees out of the payroll system, which has the ripple effect of later forcing off-cycle checks which then incurs additional processing and additional printing fees of $250 for each check. All this and more results in a weakened business partner relationship between HR and IT departments.

So how are the issues surrounding bandwidth combated? The first thing to do is take a proactive approach to planning projects, maintenance, and support around the natural peaks and valleys of HR operations. Secondly, cross-train team members to provide more flexibility in staff assignments. This will provide the ability of shifting resources during peak periods or when emergencies might arise.

Recognize trends and specific areas of SAP HR that seem to be the bottleneck and focus on those areas for cross-training. For example, if a team is consistently falling short in the area of Time Management, focus on the specific areas where the help is most needed. If the need happens to be work schedule creation, invest time in cross-training a resource in that area. This will help build up "talent reserves" in key areas to provide more coverage.

Map out peaks and valleys. These periods of alternating intense requirements and minimal activity should be factored in, reviewed, and anticipated on an annual basis. Plan accordingly. Implementing new functionality in Payroll that involves resources from the business for testing during the month of December is probably a bad idea.

Set realistic expectations around due dates. Allow more time for non-critical changes to provide a buffer for the unforeseen crises. It's also a good idea to have weekly meetings with the business to prioritize what's being worked on. This is an effective way to manage expectations and build working relationships.

Also consider using SAP HR consulting firms that specialize in production support. They can provide the variable bandwidth needed. The key for making this work is picking the right vendor. While there are many consulting companies to choose from, few are specialists in this area.

Resource Training

It is not realistic to expect one person to know everything. The rule of thumb is if anyone tells you they are an expert in every area of SAP HR, it is very possible they are exaggerating their abilities. So do not expect any one individual to know it all. This being the case, a best practice is to invest time in training resources. There are various ways to obtain training including standard SAP training courses, either at a physical location or online. There are self-study methods available via books and manuals, cross-training using internal team members, and custom training in your own system from an outside vendor.

Due diligence is required for selecting training sources. There are a lot of organizations that offer training but most of the training is high level and cannot be applied to a production support environment. Production support requires more than just SAP skills. Diagnostic and analytical skills are needed as well as an understanding of the underlying business processes. Effective production support requires not only the ability to work with the system, but also the ability to work with people.

Standard SAP training is comprehensive, but much of the material may not apply to your organization. For example, if you are not using standard posting to accounting in payroll, there is no need to be trained on this function. Your processes may change in the future, but when they do two years after the training, retaining will be required.

Conferences are not the best source of training, although they may sound appealing. SAP HR conferences are great for exploring other ways of doing things in the system, learning from the mistakes of others, and getting updates about the latest and greatest functionality. Conferences, however, don't get into the level of detail really needed, like learning how to configure garnishments. You may get some tips and tricks which is good information to have, but it is not enough information for analysts to effectively provide real-world production support. There is no concrete data that can be taught or understood in an informational session that is sixty minutes long minus fifteen minutes for questions.

Limited staff time and limited travel budgets always get in the way of having a comprehensive training program. This, however, doesn't negate the importance of training. It is hard to stay up to speed on the latest functionality when only viewing your current system every day. At the same time, it is difficult to gain efficiency with rarely used skill sets.

The best training you can get is in your own system. This allows you to focus on the functionality that your organization uses within SAP HR and also focus on the recurring maintenance activities. This is an area where a production support partner can make significant contributions. A qualified partner will have the resources and expertise to develop a custom training plan based on your organization's specific needs, current situations, or planned upcoming events. For example, rather than providing generic Payroll Schema training, your outside partner can develop the course in a way that uses your schema rules during the training instead of using a generic schema that may not fit your scenario. This training is much more effective because the analysts apply the lessons to real issues.

Another great source of training is your own team. This includes creating a comprehensive cross training plan. Create reusable training materials so if you do have new resources on the team in the future, you don't have to rebuild the wheel. Shadowing and mentoring is another great way to get team members up to speed.

"On the project" training is another method we recommend. This involves getting your team members actively involved in projects that are deploying new functionality. The key term is "actively involved." This takes effort from all parties involved. If you have a third party implementing the new functionality, they must be a true partner and embrace their role in resources development. Additionally, management has to free up the resource from their day-to-day assignments in order to work on the project. An effective model is assigning internal resources as dedicated full time project team members and using your production support partner to backfill routine day-to-day production support activities. The goal is that after implementation, internal resources will have the skills needed to support the new functionality.

One final area of resource training often overlooked is end-user training. A large amount of production support issues arise from incorrect use of the system. It is best practice to provide regular end-user training, especially when there are either new users or key processes are involved.

Managing Turnover

There are a number of reasons people leave an SAP HR support organization, including stress, transition to consulting jobs, retirement, or job dissatisfaction. Whether it's leaving the company or an internal transfer, employee turnover can easily disrupt service levels when it comes to supporting SAP HR.

Unplanned turnover places a burden on existing resources that are required to pick up the slack until a replacement is found. Planned turnover may in some cases avoid this burden with proper foresight, but whether unplanned or planned, employee turnover impacts the ability of the organization to meet service level requirements.

In some cases the structure of your IT department may be a catalyst that accelerates turnover. Employees in break/fix roles may feel like they are stuck in dead-end jobs with little hope for advancement. One of the keys for reducing turnover is keeping your team challenged.

Consider the true story of a former colleague who took an in-house support position to get off the road from her consulting travel. Within six months this person resigned and went back to her independent consulting job. The consultant was not challenged in the support position and felt she was caught in the trap of putting out fires. The final straw was when the business wanted to implement e-Recruiting and denied her the opportunity to work on the project because they could not afford her to be away from the day-to-day support job. Her only option was to sit back and watch outside consultants do the "fun and challenging" work, or resign from the position.

The reality is IT turnover is a fact of life. The reality also is that it can cripple an IT organization responsible for supporting SAP HR. All too often organizations rely heavily on that one superhero who knows the system inside and out. When that person leaves, the organization has a problem; they have to start from scratch while delivery suffers.

In recent years some unusual trends have taken shape. Prior to the recession when there were a lot of new SAP HR implementations underway, an increased number of internal IT resources were leaving stable corporate jobs to venture out into the consulting world. As time progressed many "road warrior" senior consultants were out of work due to the recession and with hat in hand, they accepted "in house" jobs to stay employed. When the economy and job market for SAP HR picked back up, they began returning to the consulting world. This again leaves a huge gap in several organizations' HR IT departments.

This brings us to topic of SAP I.P., or Intellectual Property; this is the knowledge your analysts have of your business users, technical details of your SAP HR system, and an understanding of the SAP HR related business processes. Unfortunately, most organizations do not have much of these areas clearly documented, which increases their vulnerability when turnover does occur. The more customized the SAP HR environment is, the more serious the vulnerability becomes.

Production support is an area where documentation is critically important. Documentation is not restricted to the initial system blueprint and configuration. True SAP I.P. evolves with the documentation of each issue and maintenance task. The problem is it's difficult to get analysts to document their own work; human nature just makes it that way. Yet, without documentation organizations and consultants will ultimately find themselves in deep trouble at the worst possible time. Good documentation doesn't only speed issue analysis and troubleshooting. It will also reduce issue resolution time and enable routine tasks to be offloaded to other resources, thus reducing the dependence on that "superhero" always being available.

Cross training is vital. It takes time to become an expert in any specific area of SAP HR. Knowledge sharing sessions, training, and good documentation are effective ways of building and spreading that expertise throughout your staff. This is yet another way of reducing turnover vulnerability. A good rule to follow is never have only one person with needed expertise; always think in terms of backup when it comes to production support.

Consider supplementing your internal team with an external support partner. When done correctly, several things can happen to reduce turnover vulnerability. First, variable resources from the support partner can be used to backfill some of the routine but time consuming production support tasks, which allows your internal resources time to work on projects. This serves to broaden internal staff experience while at the same time making their jobs more self-fulfilling.

Second, if you use resources from your support partner to implement new modules and add new functionality to the system, let your internal resources team with these experts and learn from them as they work side by side. This on-the-job training will ultimately make on-going production support easier for your in-house team.

A third way an external support partner can reduce turnover vulnerability is by documenting the knowledge transfer that takes place as they become operational in your support model. This knowledge repository then becomes a part of your formalized SAP Intellectual Property.

Creating True Business Value

Production support has two dimensions. One dimension involves issue resolution and keeping new system releases and updates current. This is commonly referred to as Break/Fix and Routine Maintenance and is primarily reactive in nature. It's pretty straightforward; something breaks in the system, meaning a business process is not able to be completed or erroneous results are being produced, or SAP has issued changes that need to be implemented in the system. This work is very important but these efforts get very little recognition from the business.

The second dimension deals with projects, major change requests, and process improvements. These efforts include implementing new functionality within SAP HR. They also deal with enhancing the current system to provide process automation and efficiency for the users. This work, more proactive in nature, is also very important and gets the highest recognition from the business.

Most organizations, however, spend most of their time dealing with break/fix issues and routine maintenance. While this is a necessary evil, most HR users want to see higher value results, usually in the form of adding new functionality and enhancements. The key to shifting the balance from reactive to proactive services is stabilizing your production support environment, which will reduce the occurrence of break/fix issues. This then frees up the resources with the most knowledge of your business, processes, and users to work on higher value process improvements.

Just think about it. Business users don't go off to major SAP HR conferences every year and come back saying "I can't wait for my IT department to fix something" or "I can't wait for them to generate next year's holiday calendars." They want the latest and greatest SAP HR functionality to make them more competitive in the HR space. They want to see ways of making their jobs easier.

Creating more business value begins with stabilizing the SAP HR system to reduce the number of problems and to reduce the amount of time spent on reactive support issues. From there, proactively work to build a true business partner relationship with HR. This involves getting involved in the formulation of HR IT strategy instead of waiting for new projects and functionality to be dictated. Offer fit/gap analysis for adding new modules or new functionality to modules that are already installed.

Conduct root-cause analysis of issues and recommend process improvements that impact the usability of the system. Provide insight on inefficient processes and look for ways to reinforce best practices. There is an upfront investment in time but it will pay off in the long run with reduced break/fix issues.

End-user training is a chance to kill two birds with one stone when it comes to increasing IT value to the business. It's a simple way to help business users to do their jobs more efficiently and to increase adoption of the system within the organization. End-user training also helps reduce issues that arise from not using the system correctly. Analyzing trends from break/fix root-cause analysis is a good place to identify training requirements. For example, the issues from incorrect Payroll Year-end Processing can linger for a long time. Analyzing what went wrong and why will pave the way for you to proactively train your users on the right way to do things, eliminating future problems.

Tracking the amount of time spent on break/fix and routine maintenance compared to time spend on projects will tell you a lot. Once you have a baseline set of data representing a three to six-month period, analyze what was actually done in both categories. This will tell you where attention should be focused to reduce break-fix issues as well as highlight any skill gaps you may have. You'll then be in a position where you can set goals, implement changes, and track progress.

Key Learnings

- The complexity of supporting SAP HR stems from the cyclical nature of human resource business processes and ever changing business, regulatory, and compliance requirements.

- Production support issues generally fall into four categories: Bandwidth, training, turnover, and value creation.

- Bandwidth refers to having enough resources at the right time with the right skills. Proper planning and setting realistic expectations are important. Using a variable resource model will help when dealing with peaks and valleys in support requirements.

- Training is an on-going process. Outside training is valuable but it is not a substitute for on-the-job training. Training should include both IT and end-users.

- Turnover can't be eliminated but it can be controlled. Keeping staff engaged with 'fun and challenging' work is a must. Leveraging external support partners is an effective way to eliminate turnover vulnerability.

- Increasing business value of IT means reducing time spent on break/fix issues and increasing time spent on enhancements and business process improvements.

- Ongoing prioritization around open work between IT and HR manages expectations and allows for better resource planning and budget forecasting.

- To add value, IT must have a business outlook. Support analysts must be given opportunities to learn both technical skills and business operations.

- Be proactive.

Chapter 2

The Fixed Priced Model

By Raaz Karimi

Fixed Price

The lessons learned from working with both "Fixed price" and "T&M" models are best described by examining various aspects of each.

If the customer has constraints of limited time and limited budget, this usually implies limited scope. A fixed price model can most likely satisfy this requirement. So would a fixed priced model be the most suitable one that lends itself to better scope management? Or would T&M be the best choice? Let's examine the advantages or disadvantages of a fixed priced model.

Advantages:

- It would be in the best interest of the implementation partner to stay focused in order to get work done on time and under budget. Any extensions with timelines would be costly for the implementer and not as much for the customer.

- The customer gets to implement software in phases. This can be planned ahead of time and defined within the statement of work.

- If additional functionality is required, change requests can be written and functionality requested.

- Customers do not have to worry about inaccurate estimates from a financial point of view. In today's business environment, some consulting firms will make various promises to win projects. It is extremely difficult to estimate work without having completed the blueprint phase of the project. Yet this is repeatedly done in which estimates are provided without detailed knowledge of requirements. Should this be the case, the implementation partner would be most affected by inaccuracies as they would need to hire additional resources or move the project timeline, both adding to their cost.

- A fixed price model works well when the scope of work is well defined.

Disadvantages:

- Customers generally have an inclination to revert back to their current business processes, whereas within SAP, the same functionality may be offered with a slight change in the business process. To keep current business processes, oftentimes, enhancements are needed to the core SAP software. If not carefully evaluated, this can lead to increased change requests and become the main reason for delays and increased costs.

- It is a great challenge to achieve the objectives of lower costs and high quality. It takes tremendous expertise in managing relationships to effectively manage the change management process and avoid scope creep wars. When there appear to be scope increases as a result of a strong push by the customer and there is no change request approved, consultants may sometimes have no choice but to cut corners, sacrifice on quality to meet deadlines, and risk having an unhappy customer. Hence, although the process of change requests is usually in place, the scope change in question is not always agreeable to both parties.

Implementation partners will try and get work done with as few resources as can be managed in an attempt to cut costs and maintain profit margins. If resources are too few, there is constant pressure to deliver on documented unreasonable deadlines, which results in unhappy members of the team.

T&M (Time and Material)

Now that we have taken a look at the various aspects of the fixed price model and can appreciate the complexities it can bring, let's examine what the T&M model brings to the table.

Advantages:

- It provides the customer with the ability to focus on specific areas of functionality.

- It reduces situations that lend themselves to scope creep disagreements, giving the customer more authority to drive decisions.

- Sufficient time can be allocated to defining requirements more accurately.

- Customers and vendors can ensure a higher quality product. Project schedules, although always aggressive, can slot in for the right amount of testing cycles, and sizing of the team.

Disadvantages:

- It can work in favor of the vendor in some cases. For example, if the customer does not provide the necessary information to the vendor in a timely manner, vendor resources that are already engaged at the customer site are still billable during that time when they are in wait mode. Keep in mind that T&M projects in their purest form are almost non-existent; otherwise this would not be a factor in consideration.

- The vendor consultants may recommend more functionality than is needed. With constant software changes there are newer ways of performing tasks and providing the new functions to the customer.

Being on top of these software changes is valuable for both customer and consultants in most cases but not always necessary. However, the customer must carefully evaluate these to avoid additional costs.

The selection of a pricing model should be based on careful examination of objectives such as scope, time, budget, and quality. If dealing with a fixed priced model, delivery requirements and quality acceptance criteria must be clearly defined, and change management should be under control. If dealing with T&M, the customer has to ensure that unnecessary add-on work is carefully contained in order to avoid delays and unplanned costs.

There are instances where both models can work just as well. For example, production support and maintenance tasks can be handled well using T&M or a fixed price model with a well defined SLA agreement.

Resources

When staffing a team of contractors, the candidate selection process is a critical component to ensure the success of an implementation.

Important things to consider when selecting individuals for short-term contracts don't differ too much from the criteria we use to select permanent employees. Technical knowledge, problem solving skills, commitment to work, team player, and soft skills are all required regardless of which type of employment. These things, however, often seem to be ignored when hiring contractors.

So what does it take to make sure that you have the best selection process possible? An understanding of the technology, how it has changed and evolved over the years, and a grasp of the broader picture and the landscape are all keys to efficient selection. These are things that a consulting firm would posses but too often are well outside the capabilities of a recruiting firm, which forces them into one of two scenarios: Conduct interviews based on buzz words found on consultants resumes or contract out the interviews to be performed by other consultants. The cons of conducting interviews by such means are:

1. No ownership in the process
2. The risk of eliminating a viable experienced candidate as they may have missed a couple of industry buzzwords on their resume.

Other factors that have a negative impact on the selection process by recruiting firms are time to hire/close, duration of the contract, and the availability of individuals, but the biggest impact is driven by the financial component. Recruiters' main objectives are to find candidates with the lowest quotes in order to maximize their revenue. Obviously this means that the primary emphasis is on dollars and not necessarily the best candidate.

The lesson here is that there are no short cuts during selection and all resources should be evaluated thoroughly to ensure building of a good team. For consultants, build a solid network and produce solid references. Prepare thoroughly for any interview, but keep in mind that the interview process is largely about creating a favorable perception.

Training

The training of consultants (employees) is an area that is overlooked these days due to financial reasons. The short-sighted objective of having consultants billable from day one seems to supersede time invested in training, which is necessary to ensure the long term success and growth of the consultant and the consultancy practice.

Some of the compelling reasons for training are:

- Continuing education for experienced resources to transition into newer technology in order to be able to support existing customers and drive new customers.

- Training classes need to be more focused on the practical aspects of the tasks associated with an implementation rather than generic concepts. Using real life scenarios for developing training material is far more effective than an abstract concept-based curriculum.

- Having trainers with real life project work experience is important as there is no substitute for experience, and a classroom instructor alone will simply not have the depth to get consultants ramped up effectively and in time.

Communication

One of the most common success factors known to us all is good communication. Yet it is one of the most difficult, and poor communication is possibly the biggest reasons for subpar success. So what are the various aspects of good communication?

Good communication is open, respectful, patient, to the point, and multicultural. Just being able to communicate in the same language does not qualify as good communication as I have noted on some projects. The inability to communicate well is a result of fear, insecurity, lack of knowledge, and most times lack of desire. It takes serious effort to be a good communicator, but if one cares enough, then it becomes easy.

Open communication: When team members feel comfortable openly sharing information amongst each other without fear of being judged.

Respectful and Patient communication: When team members are considerate with each other and trust and respect each other, their emails and spoken words will reflect that. Oftentimes, proper email language and tone are neglected even by the most experienced.

Effective (to the point) communication:

- How much is enough? Is it relevant? Who is the target audience?

    - More communication is better than less. Not all of us can be to the point every time. Topics that have more complexities will make it necessary to do more rather than less.

    - The email titles often do not match the content in the email. What is not realized is the amount of cumulative time that gets wasted. For example, if you receive a significant number of emails in a day, you are bound to ignore an email with a title that does not have any relevance. Hence, unnecessary delays will occur. Although this issue applies to any type work, it is more significant for SAP implementations that involve immense coordination between various team members with various backgrounds and responsibilities, and above all with the fixed duration of projects.

    - We all know that our communication should be tailored based on our target audience. However, there are still a lot of irrelevant emails and spoken words.

Multicultural: Cultural differences in a global environment influence the type of communication and interaction.

Being aware of these and attempting to acquire a deeper understanding of these differences is extremely important and helps improve the communication process. The difference is notable on projects that are global as opposed to ones that are country specific. The common mistake made by some individuals is when they think that there is only one method of communication which should be understood by all others. Rather than sticking to one approach, we must be open to understanding and constantly adapting to new ways. This also helps us focus be on being part of a solution and not the problem.

Selecting the right consulting firm to perform the work

"You get what you pay for" is exactly that. I have heard of several failed projects and although all blame cannot be laid upon a consulting firm, the higher percentage of it should be borne by them. Throughout my career, I have seen that having the right company that can provide you the right team is the best way to succeed. Perhaps in the near future we will all use the ALL About Collaboration forums where there are forums that can rate consulting firms and clients can use this information to pick the right company. If independent consultants are held to high standards, why aren't the consulting firms that claim to provide services held to the same standard? Being protected by contractual agreements is after the fact and still costly. Why not spend the time in the beginning to see through the smoke?

Chapter 3

The Four Quadrants of a SAP Learning Project

By Tracey Grooms

Whether you are the client or consulting partner there are four quadrants to consider when implementing a learning project. Whether or not the implementation is internal or through a consulting partner, the role of the system integrator is consultant. This consultant role also applies to external learning suppliers.

Determining where one stands in the Learning Life Cycle is determined by evaluating your position in the transformation from training to learning. The concept of training to follow directives has evolved to applying training or learning.

Content is as unique as the content creator. To increase course offering by increasing writers and software offering adds to the complexity of a learning project. Finally, in this time of limited resources metrics are required to justify investment in learning projects. To optimize these factors on a particular implementation requires collaboration and patience. Matching these collaboration partners based on the four quadrants below is critical to picking a vendor, defining the scope of your project, and remotely being successful.

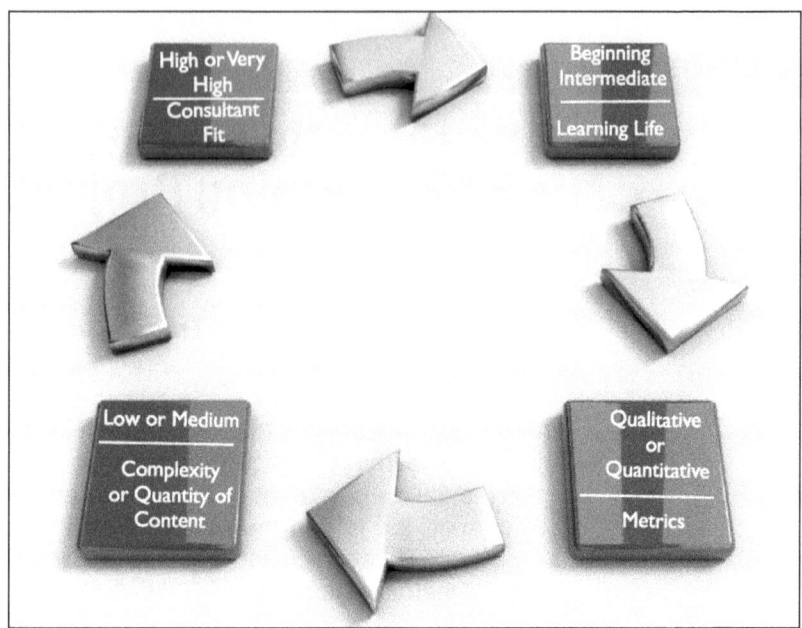

Figure 1: Four Important Quadrants of a Learning Project

Let's assume the basics: You are competent, command the proper skills, and know that your week is not forty hours regardless of what method of reporting is used. When you are involved in learning you eat, think, and drink the components most of the day. Where else can you work and get away with looking at activities around you and ask "How does that affect my work?" Everyone thinks you are last but you know that you are the linchpin of HR.

Learning does not fit the mold of the classic HR RFP or RFQ. The shorter the time put in the requirements or replies, the higher the probability of failure. A global learning system does not mean one size fits all.

Consultant Fit

Just because your implementing partner is knowledgeable in his/her area does not mean your consultant understands the client's business. Public, private, and not-for-profit operations fund capital and expense projects differently.

Learning involves human perception and interaction. Both you and your consultant should be able to apply human resource guidelines in terms of compliance and fairness. How can a consultant integrate learning with other factions of an organization if they are not an integrated consultant?

Learning is now recognized as a spoke in the wheel of Talent Management. The Talent Lifecycle begins before recruitment, continues during employment with daily operational processes, policies, performance measurement, process improvements, and succession plans. It then continues through retirement plans, layoff benefits, COBRA offerings, health plans, wealth plans, and pensions. Your learning system is not only expected to handle these topics, but it is also expected to have a life expectancy greater than other HR modules.

If you are considering being a learning consultant, you should ask yourself the following questions. Are you the right consultant for learning? Will your skills and experience compliment the client's skill set? Do you have the patience to wait for a decision or the energy to return to a decision point and start over with a smile? Can you find success for your client with an engagement that has a high probability of change?

The criteria for selecting an implementation consultant ranks from "High" to "Very High." High indicates that the organization has a comfort level with the complement that the consultant brings to the project. Very High indicates that there is a match between the consultant's capabilities and the operations of the organization. Organizations may go for the low price supplier, but their criteria require that the partner have at the least a high level of competency. The assumption is that if the organization cannot find a consultant with high competencies, then the purchasing decision will be either redefined or deferred. Medium and Low competencies in a consultant are risky.

"Learning Life Cycle" in the Organization

Similar to the Product Life Cycle, learning continues to evolve beyond the infancy stage of both the observation and teacher/student phase of instruction. In the last decade various technologies reduced the labor-intensive effort of providing instruction. The training market place is changing with the primary differentiation being those that offer an exception learning experience only and those that offer the learning experience with integration with the Talent Management offering that tracks employees, contractors, and suppliers.

Similar to the market for "apps" there are many applications for learning. The number of vendors and systems resembles the market for downloadable applications to your computer. The most important criteria are the ability of your selections to sustain you through your product life cycle. System support and the longevity of the supplier is an important factor.

The other important factor is the structure and dynamics of you organization. A very important question is always: What will be the impact if our organization experienced unplanned expansion or shrinkage? The concept of acquisitions and divestitures is always a challenge in the learning organization.

For example: SAP Training and Events, SAP Learning Solution, and SAP Enterprise Learning have been in the marketplace for over a decade. The product has evolved from a classroom scheduling only to an expansive offering of virtual learning.

The categories picked for this quadrant are low and medium. In the past few years the contraction of the world economy and the rapid expansion of technology raised the bar on the abilities of a learning system. The concept of virtual learning in terms of learning from a distant location and the use of simulations has expanded the reach to users and customers.

To be a master of teacher-to-student learning only with the ability to use technology to reinforce concepts is a "low" rating. A rating of low indicates that there is recognition of the continuous improvement process. To move in the direction of medium warrants efficiency in application, rapid change, and flexibility in delivery. For a product in its infancy a rating of low or medium would be considered as good.

Continuity of Content

Learning content is any material that is shared with the learner. There is the standard hard copy that historically was placed in spiral bound notebooks. The second included soft copies of material and/or simulations.

A learning consultant may not know the all of the concepts of a content writer's skill set, so it takes collaboration with a network to figure out client made courses. There are at least a dozen organizations that reference content guidelines, but the most critical exercise is to understand the organization's current inventory of content and any anticipated purchases.

A necessary and preventive measure for organizations is for the learning department to partner with the purchasing department to develop future content purchasing guidelines. These guidelines should adhere to the system capabilities of learning guidelines of your organization. Consideration of a content packaging vendor or toll may be a viable cost savings measure.

The criteria of low or medium are used to measure content. The concept of online or virtual content delivery has enhanced learning. This particular concept of online delivery has shifted the capabilities of going from training to learning in the past decade. If your content is still in spiral notebooks and has yet to be interactive, consider your offering within the Belle Curve and rate your organization as low. If you now know the perils of content and rely on your network of subject matter experts to address business concerns, rate yourself as medium.

Metrics

Learning increases engagement. Engagement is assumed to be and to yield identifiable results that justify investment into a learning project. Learning engagement develops behaviors and skills that give an organization a competitive advantage. The charge of the organization is to determine the level of engagement need that would provide an expected return. To measure this expected return, metrics are required for learning.

Obvious areas for metrics are safety, accounts receivable, presentation skills, inventory management, and payroll activities. Once items are prioritized and determined comparable a direct relationship between learning and engagement can begin. If returns are difficult to identify, the metrics do not correlate, or decisions are based on subjectivity, the degree of difficulty can be exponential. The intangible and high return items such as ROI, market value, ROA, EBITA, and customer loyalty are desirable but uniquely measured depending on organizational structure and systems.

These metrics impact the probability or criteria for funding. The funding method can drastically impact the scope and measurement of success of a learning project. For example, the public sector has a specific amount and timeline for spending. Private industry operates on more the budget and percent of completion. Not-for-profit is similar but needs to meet budget guidelines or reductions based on actual cash.

To measure metrics, the two approaches are qualitative and quantitative. Qualitative places the decision of rating the effectiveness of learning based on an identified criteria done by a subject matter expert. Quantitative measure is statistically based. Learning being in its infancy stage has yet to develop industry accepted qualitative ratios.

In summary Learning Projects are rising on the product curve. When an organization accesses both their internal and external resources they increase their probability of success. Learning Partners should offer more than just learning experience because learning is part of Talent Management. Content is as unique as are the individuals that created the course unless guidelines are developed. Lastly, metrics are currently qualitative, but there is ongoing effort to shift to quantitative measures.

Chapter 4

Overcoming Post-Go Live Resistance to Change

By Steven Chihos

"Where you stand on an issue often depends upon where you sit."
Steven Chihos

Picture this: The SAP project is over. The consultants have left. The team has disbanded and the big implementation budget has dried up. Like sand through an hourglass, the milestones of your implementation schedule came and went. You're live on SAP, but the stakeholders are still not happy, while you and a small band of brave souls are left holding the bag for the ERP in your organization.

Sound familiar? After serving as the "Org Change Guy" on several ERP implementation and upgrade projects, I can say that this scenario is surprisingly common. "*The Post-Go Live Blues*" may also be manifested in lingering questions like:

> *"What went wrong?"*
> *"Was SAP worth all the trouble?"*
> *"What can we do now?"*
> *"Where do we even start to fix this situation?"*

If this all rings a bell, I'll begin by telling you that your situation is typical.

Most implementation projects deal with a certain amount of post-Go Live resistance to change. Anyone who tells you their ERP initiative went off without a hitch is either blatantly lying, extraordinarily lucky, or had considerably more resources to handle stakeholder resistance than you did. Take comfort in the fact that others have successfully resolved these challenges. In this chapter, I'll share how you can turn things around.

To get started, here are six forms of stakeholder resistance that often remain once the smoke clears from your big SAP initiative:

- Users insist that the system really doesn't work.

- Stakeholders still don't buy the rationale for SAP or trust the people who brought it in.

- People complain about a lack of communication and poor user support.

- Users still don't feel confident in their SAP skills.

- Employees don't see how SAP fits into the company's future.

- It's simply not in their interest to support SAP... At least not yet.

In my experience, the most effective way to tackle this resistance is to:

- Recognize the resistance for what it is based on what you see and hear.

- Address the resistance with specific actions.

- Circle back and adjust your approach as needed.

Here's how these three steps could be used to resolve each form of resistance:

Users insist that the system really doesn't work!

What You'll See or Hear: Listen for complaints about genuine defects and anomalies that negatively impact a stakeholder's ability to do their job. Watch for unexpected system behavior, technical glitches and slow response time. Since most members of the original implementation team will have returned to their regular jobs, some permanent ERP support structure will be needed.

What to Do: Let's face the facts. Complaining about defects isn't really resistance: It's an honest plea for help to address a stubborn negative reality. The first thing to do is catalog the defects, prioritize them by end-user impact, and start to address them head-on. Establish the strongest support team you can stitch together using the resources you have. Avoid panic and follow a diligent process for testing fixes before pushing them into production. Releasing unproven fixes may make things worse!

Follow-Up: As things settle down, it can be cathartic to execute a formal "lessons learned" process. Also, communicate regularly with your stakeholders about your progress resolving specific defects. Be on the lookout for "*analysis paralysis*"—*where people continually complain about a resolved problem without having tried the solution.* The Bottom Line: Dealing with other forms of resistance will be ineffective if you don't fix the system first.

Stakeholders still don't buy the rationale for SAP or trust the people who brought it in.

What You'll See or Hear: Listen for a lack of confidence in the SAP solution. People may tell you they don't think the benefits are worth the investment. They may question the timing of your rollout. They may even fear that the change has made things worse. Classic expressions of this resistance include:

"We are so different that SAP cannot possibly work for us."
"You fixed the wrong thing."

> *"We may have needed to adjust the process a bit, but this big system was not needed."*

You may also see other subtle signs of resistance such as delays in completing training, unnecessary use of process work-arounds, or utter silence from the strongest SAP opponents when you ask them for feedback. Stakeholders may also express a feeling of having been manipulated into supporting the project early on only to find that it was much harder to adopt SAP than they were lead to believe. I once had a client say they felt they had been *sold* on the idea of an ERP rather than having been allowed to "*buy into it*" on their own terms. This perceived lack of opportunity to shape their own future is often described as "*having been handed a done deal.*"

What to Do: Create ways for stakeholders to influence priorities for future ERP enhancements without giving the perception that you can undo past decisions. Restate the SAP rationale in case anyone missed a key portion of the business case, but don't linger on it. Be honest about lessons the team has learned since Go Live, but be clear that the time for implementation project decisions has long passed. Most stakeholders who need something more from SAP will be eager to participate in defining future requirements.

Follow-Up: Keep the lines of communication and trust-building open by allowing regular feedback through surveys, site visits, and town hall discussions. Pick a few key business metrics and track them as a part of regular business status reporting. Finally, collect adoption metrics and analyze them to determine which organizational units are struggling most to accept SAP and focus your efforts there.

Complaints about a lack of communication and poor user support.

What You'll See or Hear: You could hear everything from panic, exasperation or ambiguous concern to total silence. You may not hear anything unless you actively seek feedback. The lull that comes after a big project can make some stakeholders feel out of touch. When faced with a lack of information, people often "*fill in* *the blanks*" based on what they know, what they want, or what they fear is the worst-case scenario. In many cases, users will "phone a friend" for help rather than use the official support channels due to a lack of confidence in the support team's ability to help them in a timely manner.

What to Do: The end of the project signals a great time to realign messaging channels. For example, most of the news about SAP during the implementation project came from the team, the sponsor, and the training folks. In the post-Go Live world, communication about the technical aspects of SAP should come from the ERP support team while communication about how business processes work in SAP should come from the business functions that run on SAP. Use active communication methods such as online town halls and passive methods like self-service websites. Include brief ERP updates in recurring status meeting agendas. Be as forthright as possible while avoiding the urge to "spin" communications to suit a rose-colored view of events.

Follow-Up: Leverage a "champions network" of users to verify that messages are getting deep enough into the user base. Circle back with those who expressed concern and get tangible feedback. Don't settle for generalities when people complain. Dig deeper into issues to make sure they are valid concerns and not just frustration. Promise to listen, but don't promise to unravel business process changes. Promise to hear, but don't commit to reconfiguring your ERP. It could be that resistors only heard those parts of the business case that they wanted to hear the first time around. It could be that they've successfully resisted past changes by blustering. The key technique in either case is listening. Many users let go of their resistance once they've had input into the situation.

They still don't feel confident in their SAP skills.

What You'll See or Hear: Listen for expressions of low confidence at the personal level. Sometimes this concern is rooted in a failure to complete the training for a given user's role or a mismatch of learning styles between users and training providers. Stakeholders may express being overwhelmed and use phrases like "*there's been too much change, with too little time to adapt.*"

What to Do: Put the cookies on the bottom shelf. As you address individual readiness concerns, keep the assistance easy to understand and take your time explaining things. Engage a network of user champions to draft Frequently Asked Questions (FAQ's) and cheat sheets to be hosted on a website as you fill learning gaps with supplemental training materials. Actively seek questions and find stakeholders willing to demonstrate how they use the new system in their daily routines. Create a "Sandbox" to make it easy for users to try out the system in a safe environment where they can't destroy their real data. Picturing oneself actively using SAP—even in a practice scenario—can be critical to helping them believe they will make it through the adoption process.

Follow-Up: Monitor user confidence and give people as much time to adjust as your business model allows. Emphasize which skills have the highest priority and communicate when users will be expected to be "up to speed" with SAP.

Employees don't see how SAP fits into the company's future.

What You'll See or Hear: People respond more positively to a change if they can picture a compelling future state. If no one in a position of leadership or cultural authority has painted this picture, permission to resist may be implied. Some stakeholders may doubt that the organization has the necessary resources to support SAP along with other strategic priorities.

What to Do: Have leaders and managers of different business functions continuously re-iterate how SAP fits into the company's future. I once had a CEO describe their new ERP as a necessary toolset to move their company from #21 in the world into the Top Ten in their market space. The Vice President of Sales, the CIO and each Director could describe in specific terms how the ERP would help them achieve their part in reaching that global goal.

Follow-Up: Employees don't always ask for strategic direction, but they can sense it when it's missing, so make sure that any future SAP improvements are tied into your organization's annual strategic planning process. Create a network of champions from among the user community to provide input on how SAP could be leveraged strategically and have them sanity-check how well the company's vision for SAP fits into their reality.

It's simply not in everyone's interest to support SAP—at least not yet.

What You'll See or Hear: Most ERP support teams hear lingering complaints that are not backed up with legitimate helpdesk tickets or demonstrated negative business process impacts. The fact that people are not dancing in the street doesn't necessarily mean that SAP is a poor fit. Sometimes people just need to vent and the newest change is the easiest target. Sometimes employees resist changes in what behaviors are rewarded. For example, if SAP uses online Goods Receipts, those who insist on using paper GR's will suddenly feel punished for doing what was once considered "the right thing." Another source of latent resistance is an ongoing fear of negative personal impact. An example: Users of your internal warehouse may be slow to adopt online direct ordering from external vendors because they fear the internal warehouse may become obsolete and the people who work there may lose their jobs. "Process Heroes" who regularly saved the day by clearing logjams in your old process may consider the user-empowering features of SAP to be a threat to their status as problem-solvers. The bottom line: Changes to roles, responsibilities, or communication patterns can be viewed as a threat to an employee's internal political clout, personal control over their situation, or their perception of the value they bring to the organization.

What to Do: Directly engage resistant stakeholders and help them answer the question: "What's in it for me?" Communication about the demonstrated benefits of SAP may help, but make sure benefits are expressed from the perspective of each user role. For example, talk to field-level clerks, accountants, buyers, and hiring authorities to find out what real, tangible benefits they're seeing. Encourage leaders from across your organization to share how they made the SAP transition and describe how it has paid off for them.

Follow-Up: Make sure users can answer the question "What does SAP do for me?" If they can't, then you'll need to help them see the value it provides in their daily process work. Have them talk to their peers to cover both the logical and emotional bases from their own frame of reference. If all else fails, you may have to cut off access to the old processes. In the Goods Receipt example above, some users may actually wait to adopt online GR's until you make a paper GR worthless. Finally, just like with each of the other five forms of resistance in this article, the best ways to keep tabs on the needs of your user community are to employ a champions network, conduct regular satisfaction surveys, visit work locations, and hold interactive town hall discussions.

Summary

Even the most successful SAP projects can expect to face some post-Go Live resistance to change, but in most cases that resistance can be overcome with diligent follow-up. Dealing with post-Go Live defects and anomalies is simply a non-negotiable requirement if your SAP change will ever be uniformly accepted. All other forms of resistance will increase exponentially until your SAP system truly works as advertised. The longer you wait to slay this dragon, the stronger it will get.

Questions about the rationale for choosing SAP or the timing for your company's implementation are largely moot points once you have cleared the Go Live hurdle, but don't expect all stakeholders to quietly surrender their opposition—especially if the system gets off to a rocky start technically. Work with sponsors to keep the business case clearly in front of everyone and work to engage the loudest detractors in resolving their deepest concerns. Collect customer satisfaction metrics to show that your efforts are helping the users and collect business process metrics to show how SAP is helping the entire company.

Stakeholders' complaints about poor communication and support often mask deeper resistance to the SAP change. Dig into these concerns by actively seeking feedback and identifying trends that can be addressed in priority order. Discourage the use of "phone-a-friend" methods and engage champions to create content-rich cheat sheets for distribution through your Help Desk as the primary SAP support channel.

If your people are still struggling to use SAP, the solution must involve training and support. Create supplemental training materials, establish a champions network to leverage peer relationships and offer a "sandbox" environment as a safe place for people to grow their skills.

Solving the problem of how to demonstrate SAP's role in the future of your company is an easy problem to detect and describe, but solving it can be hard if you don't have access to the management and executive levels within your organization. Gather direct user feedback to help make your point and drive home the need for this key component of sponsorship.

Don't be alarmed if a few "squeaky wheels" are still having an inordinate negative impact on how SAP is viewed long after Go Live. They may have waited to get engaged because that's just the way they approach change. It may just be their way of being heard. In either case, the most effective approach I have found is to work with them directly to verify the legitimacy of their concern, then engage the loudest complainers in crafting solutions.

Closing quote:

"It's not necessarily true to say that people dislike change. It's more accurate to say people don't like being changed or having change hoisted upon them. Remember, we voluntarily go to school, take on new jobs, have kids, and move to new cities without being told we must do so to survive. The secret is to help people see how your change is in their interest, not the other way around."
Steven Chihos

Chapter 5
Lessons Learned from E-Recruiting

By Saaz Karimi

After years of working in various information technology roles I had the privilege to work for SAP as an SAP HCM consultant. My area of specialty is SAP E-Recruiting. It was exciting to be in the SAP E-Recruiting consulting business a few years ago because the product was relatively new in terms of all of the new functionality that was being delivered to customers. In addition to that I was on the largest SAP HCM project in the world! With over one million resumes that come in each year and even more applications, this system required lots of processes and details that many other SAP clients did not, which is why the lessons learned outlined here could be helpful to most organizations. I think that lessons learned from one of the largest and most complex organizations in the world can certainly be helpful to all other organizations.

For this chapter, I have chosen to discuss a few areas that would be applicable to most SAP E-Recruitment implementations.

1. Testing
2. Customization
3. Enhancement Framework

4. End-User Training and Change Management
5. Lessons Learned as Part of the Implementation Cycle
6. The Use of ALE When Implementing E-Recruitment

1. Testing: The Importance of Testing Extensively

Testing strategy should not just cover tests to verify if delivered functionality works, but should also involve scripts to try and break the system. The functional team along with super users from the customers should be thinking of things that can break down and come up with scenarios that seem unlikely. Below is an example of a scenario that was missed on an implementation even through extensive testing.

Problem: Applicants allowed to apply for a job posting saved in their favorites after the posting closing date.

Version: SAP E-Recruiting ECC 6.0 enhancement pack 3.

Description: During the test cycle it was discovered that applicants could save a job posting of their interest in their favorites and apply to it after the posting close date. SAP E-Recruitment did not have a check for this. Problems for customers can include legal issues if the system is notifying job seekers of "Application Acceptance" status and they are not being considered by recruiters due to the late application date.

Lessons Learned

- Preparation for the testing phase should hold members of the team truly accountable.
- Detailed documentation of current processes should have already been documented.

- The core team of SME's should work together with the super users to come up with various scenarios for testing. We discovered that we would not make our dates with all of them involved as intended initially. We included them in the project by giving them specific areas of eRecruiting that they would work on independently.

- Throughout the testing phase, it is necessary to revisit old test scripts to aid in writing new ones.

2. Customization: Heavy Customization Vs. Out of the Box

How much should we customize? This is an ongoing debate on every implementation. While it is not practical for customers to utilize an out of the box solution to meet their specific business needs, it is important to evaluate their current business process and view the new E-Recruitment implementation as an efficient solution. When looking at old versus new systems for the customer, blueprint sessions should focus on what features of the new E-Recruitment solution can enhance the customers business process rather than implementing all the bells and whistles just because it exists in the new software.

Lessons Learned

- Approach the new implementation as a streamlined, efficient solution to help improve the customer's current business process.

- Focus on change in business processes if necessary. The object of new software should not be to do things the old way.

- Involve super users and management from the customer to really understand what they currently do and what they expect of the new E-Recruiting implementation.

- Involve various departments. SAP's e recruiting tool is not specific to just the HR Department. The help desk, security department, webmaster and the applications department are also involved.

3. Enhancement Framework

SAP recommends the use of Enhancement Framework during implementations. Customers will reap the benefits when performing upgrades, modifications, or receiving new functionality from SAP.

Using Enhancement Framework customers can:

1. Enhance and substitute parts of SAP development objects without modifying them.
2. Avoid that changes are overwritten in the next update/release.
3. Control and own their enhancements as they will be developed in their own namespace.
4. Find it easier to get the latest industry solutions they want based on the latest SAP ERP release.
5. Have a lower TCO by having fewer systems in their landscape.
6. Have the ability to choose only the desired new industry solutions and re-use desired functionality of other industry solutions.
7. Stay on one stable release while still receiving new functionality.
8. Have the ability to separate the installation and activation of new functionality. This allows customers to install whatever they want and activate what they think they will use instead of an "all or nothing approach."
9. Be on a proper maintenance schedule and will be compliant with the latest industry regulations.

4. End-User Training and Change Management as Part of the Implementation Cycle

Stringent project deadlines and budgets often make the User Training phase a lower priority, however it is critical that the users know how to use their new system well sooner rather than later. User Training and Change Management are critical to ensure a smooth transition during the deployment of a new system with minimal business interruptions.

SAP Best Practices recommends the use of BPP's (Business Process Procedures) which basically specify detailed instructions of how to complete business processes within the new SAP application. A couple of other tools offered by SAP as part of user training and change management are SAP Tutor and ASAP (Accelerated SAP implementation) Roadmaps.

SAP Tutor is a simulation tool that can be used to create interactive training simulations and demos in the SAP and non-SAP applications.

ASAP (Accelerated SAP implementation) Roadmaps provides a proven implementation methodology roadmap. This methodology covers project management, configuration of business processes, testing, and training aspects of the implementation.

Lessons Learned

- Insufficient amount of time dedicated to training leads to frustration from end-users, super users, and the business in general.

- Lack of training makes the testing cycle more challenging as users will be conducting processes incorrectly and recording system defects when the desired result is not achieved.

- Time dedicated to change management will lead to less resistance of moving from old to new.

5. Lessons Learned as Part of the Implementation Cycle

Creating and maintaining lessons learned can be an important part of implementations. Lessons learned identifies a potential mode of failure or risk and the necessary steps required/taken to mitigate that risk. A Lessons Learned document should be maintained ongoing by the functional team. We see too many projects leave this step until the end at which time it becomes challenging to recap everything that went wrong or things that could have been done more efficiently.

Some of the vital questions that can be answered by lessons learned are:

- Is there a risk relevant to our project?
- How significant is that risk? Identify its impact.
- The steps that are being taken in order to address that risk.

Benefits achieved from lessons learned:

- Allows project stakeholders to be fully engaged in the project.
- Gives a clear indication of the business benefit achieved from the implementation.
- Provides proven solutions for repeat SAP implementations.
- Can be beneficial to the project when performing upgrades, new implementations, or system changes by identifying the mistakes so that they are not repeated.
- Can be invaluable in aiding new project team members to get up to speed quickly and hit the ground running when performing upgrades or new implementations.
- Serves as a blueprint as to why certain decisions and changes to those decisions were made during the implementation.

6. The use of ALE when implementing E-Recruitment

When implementing E-Recruitment, it is best to have it run on a separate box/instance from the core HR system. Master Data integrity and security are the two main reasons for this recommendation. ALE or (Application Link Enabling) allows the maintenance and support of such distributed systems by allowing the controlled exchange of business messages and consistent data retention between the applications. The integration of applications is achieved by accessing a local database as opposed to a centralized one. The distribution and synchronization of Master Data, Control Data and Transaction Data is through the asynchronous communications that ALE uses to read data across the distributed applications.

Things to consider when using ALE:

- As many different application areas can be set up to leverage ALE technology, it is important for an ALE consultant to assess the impact on the system as there could be other ALE connections bringing over the same data.

- The impact of performance issues arising from system load of other systems should be assessed. This impact if deemed significant can be reduced by the use of dedicated ALE application servers.

- Scheduling appropriate maintenance jobs is important to reduce the performance impact as Buffer tables and Indexes grow. Having a proper strategy and schedule will help maintain system performance in the various interfaces.

- Issues from space limitations can occur in development and test environments. In order to counter this, a comprehensive archiving plan must be in place.

- Archiving criteria must be appropriate for the given situation.

- SAP ALE error handling is managed by SAP Workflow. Workflow processing can create overhead in the system, therefore if Workflow is not being used to manage Idoc errors, it should be turned off.

- Inaccurate sizing of your system for its interfaces can cause significant issues and poor architectural decisions.

- A common problem that is often overlooked is the network between integrated systems. If there is a large amount of data being exchanged, steps must be taken to ensure that the physical network between the integrated systems is streamlined and bottlenecks are identified before any problems arise.

- If data encryption is needed, the adequate amount of encryption hardware needed must be determined.
- The number of hops between integrated systems must be minimized.
- Appropriate ALE Buffer table and Workflow table sizing is important in order to avoid issues resulting from space during data conversion in the testing and development environments.
- If ALE is being used on a large scale implementation, it is a good idea if possible to have a standardized way of doing things to help reduce implementation issues and to keep things simple.
- When considering the volumetric impact of ALE, one should consider the initial data load volume, frequency of records to be updated, and its schedule. Example, hourly, daily, weekly etc.

Benefits of using ALE:

- Distribution of data between SAP systems of the same or even different release.
- Customers performing an upgrade will still be able to continue the exchange of data without making any further adjustments or changes.
- The integration of SAP and non-SAP systems is now possible.
- The system will perform Data Consistency checks hence ensuring Data integrity across systems.
- Works as a tool for Error handling.
- Works as a tool for Synchronization and Monitoring Data transmission.

In Conclusion, I would like to state that the purpose of this article is to suggest looking at the topics mentioned above as a guide to follow during your implementation. Several projects do achieve successful go-lives without paying the utmost attention to the above, however, the point of having one successful implementation after another is to learn and improve. When customers contract implementations out to SAP consulting firms, they pay for experience, reliability, trust, and efficiency, all of which come from maintaining a vault of lessons learned and a knowledge base.

Chapter 6

Don't Reinvent the Wheel: *Explore SAP Partner Solutions!*

By Sean Mallon

In today's SAP market, an unprecedented number of talented SAP developers exist who have excelled in the industry for a number of years. These professionals honed in their expert skills through countless projects where tough gaps existed, complex solutions were discussed and discovered, and detailed functional specs were written. As a result, custom programs were developed, tested, and implemented. In most cases, the issues were resolved through SAP delivered User Exits, BADIs, and Function Modules which simply needed to be copied and adapted by the programmer. Then through editing of the code, the customization was activated, tested, and implemented. This usually met and satisfied the client's business process requirements and technical specifications. But what does a customer do when these pre-delivered enhancements are not enough and projects at key periods of testing are left paralyzed? And what do they do if a core requirement remains outstanding, which if not resolved in a timely manner could cause the project to fail?

The Value-Added Hand of an SAP Partner

The solution could be an investment in a highly regarded, but not always popular, *SAP Partner* product. These applications are developed from the same people who have been ABAPers and/or web programmers for the last five to fifteen years. Many of these experts have gone into business for themselves or are working for a software boutique shop where they are developing fixes and enhancements. In many cases they are saving projects and giving renewed life to a client's system.

Recently, this niche third-party player is growing faster than ever with close to 500 mid to small-size firms, offering close to 2,000 innovative and certified products. Couple this with thousands of other non-certified, but well qualified solutions, and the growth spurt of this ERP entity has been nothing less than phenomenal in the last five to seven years. The products offered can be broken down into three major areas, such as:

1. Industry (e.g., Consumer Products, Retails, Oil and Gas, and Pharmaceutical)
2. Business Function (e.g., Finance, Supply Chain, Human Resources, and Payroll)
3. Solution Type (e.g., Data Warehousing, Mobile, Netweaver, and CRM)

The applications supporting the above areas act as an assortment of gap-fillers, such as extensions, archives, accelerators, sync tools, add-ons, scanners, integration platforms, and even a brand new interface for the User. Here are a few examples of some of SAP Partner software in the market:

G-Connect

Provides bi-directional synchronization of Accounts, Contacts, E-mails and Calendar between Google Apps and SAP CRM and SAP ERP. Software by iServiceGlobe, Inc.

TAXOR

Provides tax departments of large organizations with an integrated, thoroughly useable platform in SAP®. TAXOR integrates the complete process of company tax treatment (German taxation) from balance sheets to returns as well as reporting. Software by IKOR Management.

Smartsoft Barcode Scanning Solution

Provides mobile application developers with embeddable code that scans a code, decodes that code, and puts the resultant value into a field in the developer's application. Software by Smartsoft.

Content Archive Service for Cloud

Lets SAP users use Storage as a Service as an ArchiveLink repository. The service allows a direct connection from the SAP archiving layer to major public cloud providers such as AT&T Synaptic Storage as a Service, Amazon S3 and Google Cloud. Software by Dolphin.

These types of software components can be found in places such as *SAP Eco-Hub*, which acts as an extensive on-line library of certified products by Industry, Line of Business, and Technical Solution with search capability, descriptions, reviews, and specs. However, it does not include non-certified products, which in many cases is developed by certified consultants who simply lack the funds to advertise and market their products.

So, how does one go about finding non-certified applications? Plus, can a client really rely on reviews from a subjective website such as the one offered by our friend, *SAP Eco-Hub*? And what about a comparative analysis with reviews (i.e. good and bad) from other users and clients? The answer is research, and most importantly, due diligence from within and expertise from an outside party.

To give additional insight to this world of *SAP Partner* products and their value-added solutions, I have provided a scenario below of a company that has a system gap with no viable "out of the box" solution to provide an answer to a major challenge. In addition, I provide suggestions for a client on how to avoid misuse of internal resources and actively search for external products.

A Client's Gap and Inept Solution

Phase: *Realization with integration testing set to start and ready to go into full swing.*

Requirement: *Create HR data which resembles the client's real master data, organizational structure, and payroll results along with protecting the employee's private data (i.e. Name, SSN, and DOB) through a masked mechanism.*

Issue: *Lack of a data cloning tool to support the above requirement.*

Consultant's Recommendation: *Reach out to the SAP HCM market and purchase a data cloning tool with complete documentation, training, and vendor help-desk support.*

In the above scenario, the client was facing a major obstacle: Attempting to create a mass amount of secure data at the infotype and cluster level for the purpose of testing and training. To make this happen, the customer considered the suggestion of the outside consultant along with looking at some of the standard tools in SAP, such as system refreshes, a brand new client, e-CATT recordings, and/or data loads by Infotype (e.g., addresses, basic pay, and health plans) with spreadsheets as the data source.

The common problems with the latter solutions were as follows: Private data would not be masked, time evaluation and payroll results would not be up to date, and most importantly, the master data and organizational structure would take too long to download from one client and reload to another one. Even though these potential issues were quite evident, the customer at the executive-level went with infotype data loads from a standard but limited transaction. Without truly understanding the power of a third-party tool, they ignorantly thought they were saving time and money by taking care of the data issue with an internal and untested solution.

Disaster was pending! For instance, on the day integration testing was set to begin only about 20 percent of the data was loaded, not to mention it was out-of-date, non-secure, and not very clean.

A Valuable Lesson

As a result of this crucial mistake, the client ended up delaying testing and training along with extending a previously overzealous go-live date. Hence, by relying on a standard and inept solution, key people on the projects were reprimanded, and in some harsher cases, demoted or terminated. In hindsight, if the executive had simply listened to his consultants and gone the *SAP Partner* route all of this could have been avoided. These paths to enlightenment can lead to the strategic utilization of a boutique-shop or specialized wholesaler.

The Roads Less Taken

The Boutique Shop

To resolve this project-breaking issue and to keep from spending an enormous amount of time and money to design a standard but inept solution, the client should have looked to the outside software market. For instance, it would have been wise to take the time to study and purchase a *data cloning* product that fitted their project testing and training needs. This could have been as easy as doing a search on Google or better, going to an end-user conference, such as ASUG or SAP HR and visiting a vendor's table. Normally, these booths are full of boutique-type salesman accompanied by a product expert who is there to answer potential client's questions. For instance,

"Do you have products that can copy and clone master data and organizational structures on the fly, so we can accelerate testing and training without sacrificing the privacy of the employee's data records?"

Considering the wide availability of a *data cloning* product, the client will more than likely get a "Yes" along with a brief demo of not just the product in question, but the vendor's whole suite of HCM applications. For example, the demos might have included specialized payroll tax reports, conversion tools, pre-delivered interfaces (e.g., HIPPA), and web-based portal products, such as a workflow tool for manager self-service. It is best the user not stop and chat with just one vendor. They should venture to as many booths as possible (e.g. three to five) and see other show-and-tells, collect business cards, and bring back brochures.

This is a good method to practice because when it gets to procurement-level, the rule is "the more competitive vendors on the table, the better the negotiation process." As a note, some confusion may ensue with all of these suppliers in play, but that will be resolved through RFPs, conference calls, webinars, and on-site demos. In the end, the client will be extremely educated and make the best decision, plus get a decent price on the software. Most importantly, the customer's issue will be resolved through an easy install, documentation, and training along with service work.

Examples from Top Vendors with Data Cloning Products:

Company	Product Name	Description
AspireHR	Data Architect	Enables organizations to quickly and easily generate realistic employee test data and test business scenarios that otherwise could never be tested except with the actual employee data in production.
Worklogix	HCM Data Scrambler	HCM Data Scrambler™ is a test data scrambler that creates safe, realistic, and referentially correct data that shields employee information. This product introduces pre-defined functions to apply data transformations that scramble your data.
EPI-Use	Data Sync Manager	Copies complete subsets of SAP client data or to copy selected SAP object data in ERP, SRM and CRM environments, accurately and consistently. Because it is so flexible, DSM empowers all levels of SAP users, ensuring access to production data in non-production systems for testing, training, and support.

EPI-Use Client Quote

IT Manager	"Managing non-production systems is a complicated business. We get difficult specs from business users, and the full SAP copies cause downtime. My Basis team is overworked."	"My team works less overtime, and our existing hardware is ample, so I make my budget. More importantly, with our data being up to date, our testing is faster and more accurate, so our service is better. It's a win-win situation!"

The Consultant's Role

During this exploration process, the client should consider using an outside consultant. For instance, an SAP guru who has had years of experience and deep knowledge of *SAP Partner* products along with an acute knowledge of the software firms offering them. This person can act as an objective party who will not only understand the specs, but speak to the vendors in their own technical language, help negotiate a good price tag, and be there to oversee the implementation. The money invested in this resource will be well worth it because the client can feel safe and secure in the purchasing of the product.

The Wholesale Alternative

A new concept on the horizon is the purchasing of *SAP Partner* software through a wholesale distributor. In this scenario, a customer would try this method in the hopes of buying third-party software in a bundle while at a discounted price. For instance, instead of just purchasing HR cloning software, the client would look into other areas too, such as Materials Management, Business Objects, and Portal add-ons. Basically, a cross-solution and all-in-one buy for industry, business process, and/or technical needs. Most importantly, the customer would still receive the same vendor service, but in a more controlled environment where more than one supplier would be installing and implementing software.

This wholesale process (a.k.a. e-Procurement) is still relatively young and new to the SAP Partner culture. But, if successful, it will forever change the way SAP and other ERP Partner software is bought and sold from a boutique shop to a mass market aggregator of e-Procurement services.

Conclusion

"Don't Reinvent the Wheel!"

It is an old analogy, but seems to continually apply to the world of Information Technology where smart people are developing and upgrading innovative third party products on a daily basis. However, a lack of awareness and use of these products continues to be present.

Why is this happening and how can we educate our clients?

Do it from the start! Shake hands with your potential client and within the same meeting begin to share knowledge of *SAP Partner* products. When the client states they plan to buy an ERP system with the promise it will solve all of their problems, let them know that third party certified products are part of the SAP family. For example, highlight the fact that an *SAP Partner* can enhance and extend a client's special solution along with bringing tools to resolve project challenges and issues.

Whether through a boutique shop or wholesaler, a client's industry, business line, and/or technical gaps can be filled because *SAP Partners* exists for that very reason: To go above and beyond the standard product and meet even the most extreme requirements.

Chapter 7

The Intangibles

By Jan Redmond

When I was told to write about my job, I immediately wondered how verbose I should be regarding my career. I have been extremely lucky to have such a vast career around Enterprise Resource Planning (ERP). In that instant, my thoughts quickly drifted to what I do day to day. Helping organizations determine their ERP direction is what I do on a daily basis.

So, thinking about transforming from your current backend system? Well, think again! It is not an easy undertaking. Whether you are moving from a mainframe system, AS400, or current ERP to another state-of-the-art ERP system, your backend systems evaluation becomes a paramount decision and financial commitment.

As Ben Franklin stated so well "The only two things in life that are inevitable are death and change." While change is our focus, the death part can be macabre in nature, but can be closely described as a theme if your ERP transformation has not taken the proper sequence.

Traditional ERP transformation projects tend to share the same criteria or processes centered on tangible criteria...

- Project plan worksheet
- Various ALM tools
- Blueprint session(s)
- Timeline with key dates
- Change request forms or processes
- Manage project "creep"
- Under commit and over deliver messaging (verses being accurate)

I have spent nearly the last sixteen years working for two top-tier ERP vendors and one Payroll outsourcing-type organization. Furthermore, I have gone through an abundant amount of evaluations in multiple industries throughout the globe. As of result of that experience, the LESSONS LEARNED that I have drawn from each company are noted in this chapter. To be specific, I have worked with Ceridian, Oracle, SAP, and Capgemini—all of which has been spent in the Human Capital Management (HCM) discipline.

I have been fortunate to experience ERP evaluation projects from a company with fifty employees to companies with over 900,000 employees. Those companies have been from public sector industries to oil and gas, to retail to aerospace and defense sectors. I think I have seen just about every industry over the past sixteen years. The continuum of extremes of company sizes and industries has afforded me a very broad listing of experiences—all of which have helped me gain great insight into best practices and best in class approaches to ERP evaluations.

Basically, there are three key lessons or admonitions that I would share with the next company contemplating a successful ERP transformation. These three areas are not typical or traditional criteria but drive a clear path to flawless execution of your transformation. No matter what your current state is, there are considerations that each ERP transformation must include.

Change Management: Change management is often mentioned but rarely highly associated with the ERP transformation project. Change management accommodates your company's ability to handle the new solution, new processes, and potentially new partners to your company.

Every organization must fully be aware of the enormous transformation they are about to experience. Whether it's the look and feel of the new system or the process re-engineering your company is about to experience, change will not be evaded. The colossal elephant in the room, with the name tag change, will be addressed.

Change management should be a collaborative effort between your company and the company representing the software being evaluated. There are numerous change management methodologies and most are valid. Making change management a key element to success will drive adaptability and solicit employees to embrace the change.

Change management should include quality process improvement. Allow the new technology to drive process improvement. Organizations should fully discern that they will not be doing business as usual when it comes to business processes. I am often tickled when I see evaluation requirements that require the solution to mimic "to the letter" current processes. Then that becomes the scoring criteria for the selection.

Well, that makes sense if you are merely attempting to take your current business process and leverage new technology. I guess that is like buying a new car but putting on the trade-in tires and engine in the new car.

Change management is very much a top down approach. In other words, having the senior executive endorsement sends a clear message on how the transformation should be weighted. Senior executive sponsorship eliminates the convoluted message of commitment, vision, and strategy from your organization's leadership.

Change management can almost be treated as a marketing campaign. Having a theme, mission statement, and orchestrated kickoff with key dates shared with the company sends a message to all parties not just a timeline, but drives an ebullient level of momentum for the change.

Partnership: In most cases companies are adding a new relationship and blending two different corporate cultures housed on your property. A partnership allows both companies to infer a cohabitation of people to flawlessly execute the project objectives.

Most ERP packages can address most companies' functional requirements. Once your company has determined the level complexity that the ERP solutions will support, it really determines which tier of ERP vendors are viable to support your transformation. The next critical criteria should be: Does the ERP vendor being considered match your company's values and culture.

The ERP selection should determine who will be the best partner for executing your transformation from your current state to your desired state. Vendor and Partner are not fungible terms and they do not always send a clear message to the ERP solutions people on how the relationship will be supported.

- Do they know my company-industry?
- Do they understand my strategy?
- Do they work well within my company's culture?

The partner you decide upon really needs to be committed to almost being clandestine to the project team. The solution will bring a colorful and ardent impact by itself, but the team members who are added by your partner should blend in naturally. The partner does not have to breach its identity but offer an ability to take a chameleon-type approach to adding talent to the project team.

Partnerships really need to take on a life form of their own. Executive alignment between the companies becomes imperative. Thus you will start building synergy between the transformation teams. As an example, when time, resources and funding are available, extracurricular activities can then be planned which spark bonding that is needed in order to move forward with the transformation process. The more communication is a combination of formal and informal efforts, the more commitment to mutual respect and dedication to exceeding expectations are experienced.

It goes without saying that we are individuals and the merit on which we are judges comes from what we do and how well we do it. When we think of companies, the luxury of defining a company by one individual's ethos would be careless and erroneous. A company is defined by the leadership and the sum of its employees. Keeping that in mind makes it clear that as you add companies to your 'circle of trust," you are bringing that company's credibility into account defining your company. A very verbose explanation or posture on who we partner with defines us.

People: You might think I am overstating the obvious here. To the contrary, the most powerful element in projects are the people. Our sub-plot to this chapter was intangibles, and while people are tangible, the characteristics of those individuals are commonly regarded as intangibles. People from both sides determine the likelihood of the two most driving success factors: Time and on budget.

The entire process is driven by people. People load data and people implement technology that further determines which partner (based on their people and processes) is best suited to help you be successful. However, the efforts of the persons involved allow the solution to take on the challenges in your organization.

When I mention people I mean your people and your partner's people. The evaluating company should have people who have a solid background in the company's history, the company's current processes, and the strategy to reach process nirvana. I have also noted the key character attributes that each team member should have demonstrated:

- Strong written communication skills

- Strong verbal communication skills

- Strong industry acumen

- Strong understanding of current business processes

- Strong and clear understanding of the overall project goal and mission statement

- Strong command of the project's agreed upon language for communicating

- Have demonstrated a "can-do" attitude (willingness to drive the timeline's thresholds)

- Fully endorse the project and are committed to the success of the project

When I mention people, I mean all people touching or associated with the project. If there is an offshore involvement, then those talented individuals need to be able to share information adequately. For example, any time companies present folks from the USA for a USA project but leverage offshore talent that are challenged with the agreed upon language. Having access to all *key* project participants clearly allows you to determine how well communication will be leveraged on the project.

The partner has to provide the appropriate subject matter experts (SME) to fulfill their ability to bridge vanilla software configuration to your requirements in the system. In the same breath your ability to marshal internal talent to offset the partners SMEs becomes indispensable to the project's success.

How much the team respects and decisively communicates will determine the likelihood of the project being on time.

If you revisit Stephen Covey's *The Seven Habits of Highly Effective People* published in 1989, you feel compelled to reflect on how those habits are still relevant today. I can't help but think of the habits around self. Mr. Covey mentions traits like, "Think Win-Win, Seek First to Understand, Then to Be Understood, and Begin with the End in Mind." All of the seven habits drive personal integrity and mirror the qualities in most organizations in the top ten percent.

Being that I am a HR person who has worked for many years in the ERP space, it goes without saying my diatribe on how people make the difference becomes a natural stance.

In summary, an excessive amount of time is spent on functionality; however, the above partner selection criteria are equally important if not more important. The change management and partnership criteria become essential in your company's transformation. You make a decision on a solution but equally you are adding to your company's partner ecosystem, which defines who you are as a company.

What are the underlying themes behind the two points above? They are that people will drive your company's success and the software only becomes a tool for that success. At the end of the day we ship, service, build, repair, sell, research, and market products and services to the talent level of our people versus our competitors. Our people separate one company from another. Nothing proves this more than bottled water. It's water! Something else has to be the driving factor of why we choose one bottled water over the other. In the USA, bottled water owns about 30 percent of the bottled beverage industry (Americans drink about twenty-one gallons of bottled water per capita per year, which is over ten billion gallons each year. So your marketing person has better be the best talent over your competitor.

Your ability to work together with your partner and set a clear roadmap for the path of the transformation is the Lesson Learned from my sixteen years of experience. I realize you cannot discount traditional project criteria, and these areas I have noted are often included in the project plan. My caveat is that the proper attention gets associated with these areas I have noted. Get ready for change as you add a partner and demand more of your people.

So, I leave you with the following intangible aspects to flawlessly executing your ERP project: Ready your organization for change, evaluate the company harder than the software, and ensure the resources (people) on the project are "the right people doing the right task at the right time."

Thank you!!

Jan Redmond

Chapter 8

Lessons Learned with SAP Benefits Administration

By Maxine Wood

Point One—Adjustment Reason Start Date Versus Plan Start Date in the Back Office and through ESS

These are the facts about the adjustment reason start date...

- The Adjustment Reason is the offer that will be made available to you in the Enrollment transaction.

- Adjustment Reasons are usually New Hire Eligibility, Marriage, Birth/Adoption, Change in Employment Status, etc.

- The Adjustment Reason is valid for a certain time frame. This is the time it takes for a user to enroll in or make changes to their plans using this offer.

- The Adjustment Reason has a Start Date. In configuration, you have the ability to choose Adjustment Reason Date, Date of Offer, and an Other Date.

- The Date of Offer is the date on which you create the Adjustment Reason. For example, the Benefits Department creates the Marriage Event with an effective date of 7/1/11, but it was entered into the system on 7/12/11, thus the Date of Offer is 7/12/11.

- The Adjustment Reason date is the date you tell the system the Offer can start. This usually represents the Effective Date (i.e. Marriage Date).

- The Other Date is a static date that you enter into the field in configuration.

- For Qualifying Events and Work Status Change Events, it is recommended to use the Adjustment Reason Start Date as you have more choices for processing.

- The Adjustment Reason has an End Date. In configuration, you have the ability to choose Default date, End of Time, or Other date. The Default date is the system high date of 12/31/9999. The End of Time date is also 12/31/9999.

- The Other Date is a static date that you enter into the field in configuration.

- This is not the End Date of the timeframe for which the offer is available.

- The processing days will control that and the system will automatically calculate it out for you during creation of the Adjustment Reason through Maintain Master Data. This is the end date of the plans presented with the offer. (All plans use the same end date, by the way.)

Summary on benefit plan begin dates...

Regardless of what date you choose, the Adjustment Reason start date is stored as the Begin Date of the Adjustment Reason infotype (0378) and the timeframe, also entered into configuration in the Adjustment Reason table, starts its count of days from here.

One of the biggest issues that we face when processing Enrollment in the Back Office and specifically in ESS is that the Begin Date of the Adjustment Reason also becomes the Start Date of the plans that are being added or changed with the offer; just as the End Date becomes the End Date of the plans as mentioned previously.

As an example, let's say we create a Marriage Event with a timeframe of 30 days.

When we create the Marriage Event on 7/1/11, the adjustment reason will be available until 7/31/11 (the proposed end date for this reason could also be the first couple of days in the next month if the effective date is in February, for example).

When we navigate to Enrollment using this Marriage Event, we will see the offer listed if our processing date falls in the date range given for the event.

You will notice that the proposed Start Date of the plans listed in the Marriage offer will start on the same date as your Adjustment reason, in this case 7/1/11 and they will have a proposed End Date of 12/31/9999.

If you used 7/15/11 as your Adjustment Reason Start Date, the offer will be available until 8/15/11 and when you navigate to enrollment, the Start Date of the plans listed will also be 7/15/11.

If your policy dictates that the plans should start on the first of the month following the Qualifying Event change (in this case Marriage), then you need to create the Adjustment Reason for Marriage with a Start Date equal to the first of the month following the actual effective date of the event.

In this case, the employee notifies you that they were married on 7/15/11, therefore, you will create the Adjustment Reason for Marriage with an 8/1/11 Start Date.

When navigating to enrollment, the plans will all begin on 8/1/11 and end on 12/31/9999, which is correct.

This causes some confusion with the Back Office folks, as they have trouble separating the need to enter the actual effective date provided by the employee and the date that needs to be recorded with the event in order to facilitate the correct Start Date for the plans presented for this offer. The Back Office can easily enter an enrollment processing date in the past, present, or future to get the Adjustment Reason offer to come up before it has begun or after it has expired. Of course, an expired offer usually means Retroactive processing in Payroll to adjust the employee's deductions to what they should have been in comparison to what has actually occurred.

The real issue comes into play when ESS is implemented. You want to give your employee 30 days to make additions or changes to their plans (hence the timeframe), but the Start Date of the plans has to be correct as well.

Let's review one of our earlier examples. The employee notifies the Benefits Staff of a Marriage Event. The Marriage effective date was 7/15/11 and today is 8/10/11. If the Benefits Staff creates the Adjustment Reason infotype for the Marriage event (or the employee is allowed to do so through some custom form or Guided Procedure process in ESS) on 7/15/11, the employee will have enough time to process the event (up until 8/15/11). However, the start date for the plans listed in the offer will be incorrect with the 7/15/11 start date. If the Benefits staff creates the Adjustment reason infotype for the Marriage event on 8/1/11, the employee will have more time to process the event, which in some organizations is undesirable (up to 8/31/11). However, the Start Date for the plans listed in the offer will be correct.

As stated previously, the Back Office has more control over this process because they have the ability to enter a processing date that falls in any Adjustment Reason timeframe in the enrollment transaction, thus they only need to understand their policy and manipulate the system to act accordingly. When introducing ESS, the employee needs to understand the policy (of when their plans will start based on their actual effective date), and have the ability to enroll during the correct timeframe. This particular point can be challenging as ESS only allows entries on the system date (i.e. today's date). If the Adjustment Reason is dictated by the plan start date, this changes the timeframe the reason is available to use, and if it is already expired (or hasn't occurred yet) according to the system date, the employee will have problems processing their enrollment elections.

There are usually two outcomes from the implementation of ESS:

1. Explain to the employee the timeframes they have available to them to perform their enrollment elections based on policy, and if the offer isn't available yet, they'll have to wait or if the offer has expired the Back Office will need to process the change in elections on their behalf.
2. Implement the Processing of Dates function module (PBEN0023) which will affect the Start Date of the plans correctly in relation to the Adjustment Reason start date when provided with the processing rules.

As with any function module, this is a development item that an ABAP programmer will have to work. However, you can specify that the start date of plans should be equal to the first of the month following the Adjustment Reason start date for the Marriage offer, thus allowing you to enter an actual effective date of the Marriage as the employee would recognize it, provide the correct timeframe to enable the employee to make their additions or changes to their elections accordingly, and the start date of the plans listed in their offer will all be correct. Just because you implement this function doesn't mean you can't specify in the processing rules that certain events may need to use the Start date of the Adjustment Reason infotype instead of forcing the start date of plans to a different date, which is common with the Birth and/or Adoption events.

Point Two—When to Create the Open Offer as an Adjustment Reason

SAP provides a configuration table to set Open Enrollment parameters for a Benefit Area. In this table you can define if an Open Offer is available currently or not (this controls the display of the standard Open Enrollment link in ESS), the Open Offer period (i.e. the timeframe available to use the offer), the Start Date of the plans if the offer is used, and the End Date of the plans.

In my experience the common issues with being able to use this functionality are the following:

- Organizations may have populations of employees who have separate Open enrollment periods (i.e. Different departments, Actives vs. Retirees)

- Organizations may have different Open enrollment periods for plans (i.e. Health, Dental and Life have one period, Flex Spending has another)

- Organizations may have populations of employees that are not to be offered all of the plans that they are eligible to participate in (i.e. Plans that are managed by third parties) and some organizations don't like the plans to appear if there are no permissions to process with.

In these cases, it makes sense to create an "OPEN" Adjustment Reason where you have the ability to control who gets the reason, what plan categories are offered with the reason, and the permissions that are available on the plan types associated with the reason. This method also lends itself to those organizations that need more than one Open offer to handle their needs. You can create several, for example, "OPEN" for most plans, and "OPFX" for Flex spending Open enrollment only, etc.

The Adjustment Reason is valid for a certain timeframe, which is the time you allow the user to make changes to their plans using this offer, and will serve as the Open Enrollment period timeframe.

In the configuration table for Adjustment Reasons, you have the ability to choose Adjustment Reason Date, Date of Offer, and an Other Date for the Adjustment Reason Start date. Remember this is also the Start Date used for the plans, so you will want to choose Other date and enter the Effective Start Date for your Open Enrollment (i.e. 1/1/2012). You also have the ability to choose the End Date of plans; this is usually the default of 12/31/9999 but can be an Other date, for example, 12/31/2012.

When using the Open Enrollment parameter table in configuration, you have to adjust the table and transport your changes twice per year. Once to say that the offer is available and set the Start Date and a second time to say that the offer is no longer available.

When using the Adjustment Reason for Open Enrollment, you have to adjust the configuration table to change the Start Date for the plans each year and transport your changes once.

The Adjustment Reason for "OPEN" is created on infotype 0378 for the employees belonging to the selection criteria entered into the Mass Adjustment Reason report. The date entered into this report is the start date of the Open enrollment period. When the Adjustment Reason is created, the Start Date will equal the date entered into the report's selection criteria, the End Date is proposed by reading the timeframe entered on the reason in configuration (i.e. 30 days), the Start Date of the plans will begin on the Other Date you specified in configuration (i.e. 1/1/2012), and the End Date of the plans will be 12/31/9999.

The Mass Adjustment Reason report can be found under the Group processing folder of Benefits in the SAP Menu. You do not need a configuration role to run this report tool.

Just as with any Adjustment Reason available on an employee's record (IT0378) it will also appear as available for use during the correct timeframe in ESS.

Chapter 9

SAP End-User Productivity Case Study

By LaShonda Rahming

The last few years I have had many clients ask me to conduct two types of assessments. Either the assessment is to analyze where they are today to determine what is needed in order to upgrade or implement additional SAP functionality, or they are looking for an assessment of their current issues. After conducting these assessments, it became clear that many of the issues and circumstances were common across industries and functionalities. I then began to collect various studies about end-user Productivity and marry them with my Lessons Learned documents from clients over the last ten years. From these results and interactions with SAP end-users, consultants, and SAP clients, I created an advisory board and we created an open and free platform that can be found at http://www.allaboutcollaboration.com to further support end-users. Using the platform I was now able to connect with various organizations which lead me to the idea of an SAP Lessons Learned series. This chapter will focus on lessons learned while supporting SAP end-user Productivity using Open Innovation principles.

In the following pages you will be provided with details from one organization so that you can better understand how the SAP end-user impacts efficiencies. Our case studies will focus on showing a reality that many organizations face today in a production environment after Go Live. These case studies address:

- Knowledge Management and the Lessons Learned after Go Live

- Why Performance Management was needed when evaluating SAP end-user's Productivity

- Lessons Learned concerning the strategic approach needed to execute processes that support the SAP end-user

Let's look at the statistics. According to Gartner, 76% of Users have a failing or substandard understanding of new systems software. When Enterprise system users are not given the proper guidance, they can take up to four times longer to become proficient at new job tasks and they require up to six times more support than educated users.

Information from the industry analysts tells us that most of the problems relating to application implementations are, in fact, user related. User acceptance isn't the only problem affecting project and long term success; there is also the very basic problem of user competence to use and get the best out of the system.

Lessons Learned 1: Performance Management is needed when evaluating SAP end-user's Productivity.

The following are key pieces that you should evaluate to determine how efficient your end-users are.

- Evaluation of how your end-users provide feedback to your production support team

- Evaluation of how end-users communicate themselves

- Evaluation of System Process Documents to include Test Documents, Instructor Manuals, User Manuals, Help documents, Job Aids, Websites, and Video/Simulation training

- Evaluation of the End-User Support system once an issue has been identified

- Evaluation of your Change Management process

- SAP Consultant hands on Evaluation of system that include reports, security, and license comparisons

- Production Support Cost

- Security Role, transaction, and logon information

- Workflow Health Check

- Knowledge Management Process

Case Study

Client:

This Public Sector client went live with SAP on release 4.7 and they have been live for five years.

Post Production Model

The SAP Shared Services Department is the single point of contact for all SAP related issues with its integrated Budget, Employee Self Service, Finance, and Human Resource components.

This analysis was conducted 5 years after the initial Go Live and the analysis includes the Human Resource end-user team.

Scale: 1–5 with 1 being low score and 5 being the highest score

Evaluation Questions	Evaluation Results
Platform for end-users to communicate inefficiencies	1 - Platform does not exist today.
Process to support end-user feedback	1 - Does not exist today.
Phone Line Support	3 - There is a support line and a designated process and team. They primarily support password issues.
In House Training	3 - Training does happen on a regular basis to support Portal transactions. Training documents are not organized and Business Process Procedures are not current.
Change Management process	1 - Does not exist today
Effective Reports	1 - Very few reports are being used and analytical/strategic work does not happen.
Utilization	2 - After analyzing the end-user transaction use against the security roles and current processes, end-users have found work arounds instead of using the SAP system.
Improvements made since initial Go Live	1 - No improvements were made. Only Break/Fixes were addressed.
Performance Management	1 - There is no relationship around the use of the system and the annual appraisal.

End-User Knowledge

Once this organization went live, they did not include the end-user community to help make improvements. They pushed information out but had no way to receive information from those that use it on a regular basis and usage decreased.

Innovation Platform

Their Shared Services Team did not have the knowledge to maintain the system. Two years after their initial Go Live they still had issues from the implementation that were not addressed.

Change Management

Change management was non-existent so when it was time for the upgrade there was no plan to effectively communicate with the broader community or ensure that management and project directives were aligned.

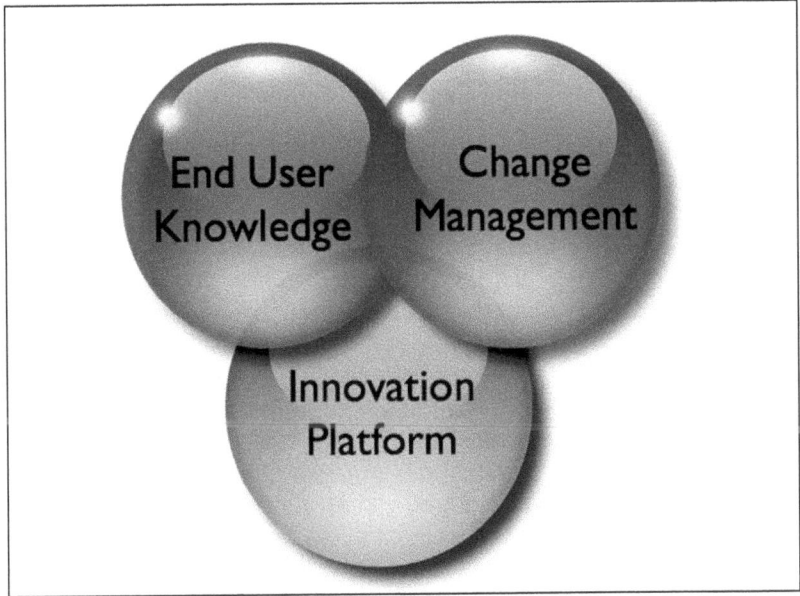

Figure 2: The image above displays how each area interacts.

SAP Lessons Learned—Human Capital Management

End-User Productivity Lessons Learned

By not providing end-users with a consistent training environment and with a voice to communicate to the support team, the end-user community has a negative opinion about the system and its features. They simply don't know how to use it. During our assessment we discovered that the system is not being utilized and that many of the users don't use the system. We also discovered that there were many offline spreadsheets that were used to get their daily work completed.

The biggest issue from the user community is that they have not been trained. After deeper analysis we found out that the shift occurred when management changed. Because the new manager did not understand SAP, they did not promote using it. Once that manager left the new manager had a team that did not know how the SAP system worked. Five years passed by and the team no longer wants to use SAP because they believe that it does not meet their requirements. After analyzing their requirements, we found that SAP does meet their requirements but they have no desire to learn how to meet their requirements in SAP as they have had a negative experience.

Knowledge Management

Change is inevitable. From the point that a SAP customer begins to use the system to the time of a significant change to that system, the people on the initial implementation will be different. Transfers, promotions, demotions, new hires, and retirement happen. These are only a few of the reasons why the team will be different. The median time spent in one job is 4.1 years.

At each point when someone leaves and knowledge walks out the door, the replacement to that position is now in a position where they many times are not as strong as their predecessor, thereby putting the new employee in a bind. What I see happen most times is that workarounds are created. Spreadsheets and changes in process occur not because the original process did not work but because the new employee is trying to figure out how to survive and thrive in their new positions. I have noticed that in the last eight years especially, when I conduct workshops that many times I hear stories like this:

John was hired into a new position as an HR Analyst in an organization that was using SAP as their HR solution. When John started he wanted to understand how to use the system but found that the documentation from the implementation had been lost and could not be found. He reached out to his supervisor who was also new and she did not know how to use the system. Her predecessor had been promoted and she did not have documentation. John and his manager worked together to develop new processes which included spreadsheets and new forms for paperwork. They used their new process and were now underutilizing their SAP HR system. One year later, the old manager came back to the department and was confused about the new processes. He recognized that the SAP HR system was not being used the way it was intended and that functionality had been lost. The team was now resistant to using SAP and he had to figure out a way to train them and update the documentation.

All of this could have been avoided if a proper Knowledge Management system was in place.

The **Bureau of Labor and Statistics** says that "Computer and mathematical science occupations are projected to add almost 785,700 new jobs from 2008 to 2018. As a group, these occupations are expected to grow more than twice as fast as the average for all occupations in the economy. Demand for workers in computer and mathematical occupations will be driven by the continuing need for businesses, government agencies, and other organizations to adopt and utilize the latest technologies. The Bureau of Labor Statistics also states that two of the fastest growing detailed occupations are in the computer specialist occupational group. Network systems and data communications analysts are projected to be the second fastest growing occupation in the economy. Demand for these workers will increase as organizations continue to upgrade their information technology capacity and incorporate the newest technologies. The growing reliance on wireless networks will result in a need for more network systems and data communications analysts as well. Computer applications software engineers also are expected to grow rapidly from 2008 to 2018. Expanding Internet technologies have spurred demand for these workers, who can develop Internet, intranet, and web applications."

With this said it means that competition will be tight and that your SAP team will change. Many organizations lose valuable information because there was not a Knowledge Management plan in place to get the information from the employee. In some cases, the employee is asked to come back to teach the team and in other cases information is just lost. With a valuable knowledge management process in place, this risk can be mitigated.

In the Era of More with Less, It Is Important to Focus on the End-User.

The increased interest of end-user organizations in having visibility into how their applications are performing—not only from the perspective of their IT departments but from the perspective of business users—resulted in more market awareness about the role that end-user experience monitoring solutions are playing in managing application performance. The market matured enough to become more aware of the fact that different flavors of technologies for monitoring the quality of end-user experience, such as those provided by Aternity, Knoa Software, Coradiant or AlertSite, do not compete against, but complement vendors such as OPNET, OpTier or Quest's Foglight.

Measuring Activities, Not Results

Ironically, many IT departments use inward-focused measures to gauge the effectiveness of their technology support. Even if they outsource support, they rely on internally-focused service level measures to monitor the outsourcing company.

A research study that Unisys conducted last year of 243 North American organizations provides further evidence of the need for CIOs to start measuring their department's real impact on user productivity which shows that end-user Productivity is starting to get some attention.

To stay competitive in today's fast-paced world, you need feedback from your end-users to connect to the people who matter most: Your employees.

A next-generation open innovation platform enables you to increase revenue, lower costs, and become more productive by delivering engaging, interactive employee experiences that transform how you do business from the inside, out.

These are some of the things that organizations are starting to implement.

Social Profiles

Enable your community users to create personal social profiles, share status updates and activities, send private messages, and share and comment on photos and photo albums.

Friend Networks

Build networks of new and existing friend connections by searching for and finding people with common interests. Connect and interact by sending invitation requests and posting on your friends' profile walls.

Discussions

Let users interact by viewing and responding to posts in threaded discussions on topics of their choice and interest. Additional features include sticky threads, tag clouds, pruning and grafting, and broadcasting.

Chat

Hold private or group discussions in virtual rooms that you can pre-configure around specific topics or allow your users to create on demand.

Ratings

Allow users to become critics by rating your content, products, or services to highlight items of interest, gain user trust, and build loyalty.

Comments

Invite people to post and view comments related to featured articles or other content, videos, podcasts, products, and services.

Blogs

Self-publish content to personalized individual or multi-author blogs and receive both ratings and comments from other users.

File sharing

Share, edit, comment, and rate documents and multimedia of all types in one central location.

Idea sharing

Capture ideas and encourage innovation by allowing users to submit ideas and then vote, tag, rate, and comment on them.

Polls

Pose key multiple choice questions and allow users to vote and view results.

Search & Browse

Make it easy for users to find the content they need quickly and with minimal effort through a series of varied search options, configurable quick links, and content tagging.

Embedded Video

Import, edit, and share rich media content (such as photos, video, and audio) across sites and within blogs, discussions, and ideas.

With this platform you will be able to:

1. Increase your return and strategic capital for your SAP Solution.
2. Lower your risks and cost.
3. Allow individuals to gain new experiences and value.

All of us can participate and reshape the story of how we interact to create custom solutions, answer questions, and solve our SAP challenges. The value is with the user entering data, the manager who needs something done, the consultant, and the executive who needs to understand. Create a platform where organizations and the global SAP community take ideas and challenges and work together to develop innovative solutions.

Chapter 10
Time Management Lessons Learned

By Michael Feast

There are many factors that determine a successful SAP Time Management implementation. However, the most critical ones can be found during the Blueprinting phase of the implementation. While some may argue that the scope of the project dictates its success, the reality is the scope can be modified, as is often the case during the Blueprint phase. The Blueprint phase is when all the requirements are gathered and documented in one place called the Business Blueprint. This Business Blueprint is not a word for word regurgitation of the employee handbook but a detailed summation of both external and internal requirements that the system will be designed to support. The Blueprint should be signed off by the relevant business process owners as a testament that everything represented in the document is accurate and there is nothing missing. This document should drive system design and be the basis for any change requests that may occur throughout the lifespan of the implementation.

A project is off to a bad start if the appropriate time and emphasis are not given to the completion and signing of the Business Blueprint. Many projects have either been delayed or have failed due to the lack of a good Blueprint. There are several components of a good Blueprint. They are external regulation, internal business requirements, and high-level business processes.

External regulations are compliance issues imposed on a company by a country's government to protect employees. In addition, regulatory bodies may impose rules and regulations that further protect employees that companies in certain industries have to comply with. It is helpful for a consultant to be familiar with a country's regulatory requirements because not all companies have knowledgeable staff to address them and therefore can be out of compliance. For instance, one company in the United States was based in New Jersey and acquired a smaller company based in California. The company's Human Resources (HR) staff was knowledgeable about the Fair Labor Standards Act (FLSA) adopted by the federal government, which stated that certain types of employees were entitled to one and a half times their hourly rate for all hours worked in excess of forty hours in a work week. However, they were not familiar with California Labor Laws that provided for daily overtime regulation in addition to the FLSA regulations. The consultant working with that company did not have any experience with implementations in California and therefore did not configure the state labor laws in the system until the oversight was caught during the testing phase of the project. The local HR resource never read the Business Blueprint and, of course, never signed it.

Fines can be levied against a company if it is not in compliance with country specific regulation. Therefore, it is imperative that a company has someone on staff who is familiar with the requirements. This is especially true of global implementations in which the company may operate in several different countries. There can be laws that range from governing regulatory reporting, leave entitlement, and overtime to the types of data to be kept. Most of the time, these laws are written in the official language of the country. The challenge and key to compliance is to have a resource for each country who is responsible for communicating (either verbally or written) these requirements in the native language of the implementation team.

Regulatory bodies are another source of external regulations. These include organizations that impose regulations that protect the integrity of an industry and/or the customer base it serves. For instance, a power company has to justify its costs in order to get approval from a regulatory committee to increase rates to its customers. This justification may entail providing proof of how much time its employees are spending on service calls, what type of equipment is being used, and how closely management is monitoring the whole process. This, in turn, means that the SAP system has to be set up to capture time against service orders as well as charging equipment time (e.g. types of vehicles, generators, etc.) against those orders. The time captures have to then show what manager has approved the time allocation and when. These requirements have to be clearly spelled out in the Blueprint. If not, the system may not be set up to properly capture or adequately report on these events. The chances for success in complying with regulatory bodies go up by having a consultant who is knowledgeable and experienced in the industry in which the company operates. The reason for this is that sometimes the business process owner deals with these requirements on a regular basis and may view them as a given—almost second nature—and fail to communicate all requirements to the implementation team.

Internal requirements are those requirements formulated by the company itself. They include items like giving premium payment for working night shifts, granting time off for vacation, etc. Here again, it is imperative to document these requirements in the Blueprint in a clearly defined and detailed manner. While each company has its own unique business requirements, most adopt best practices in order reduce costs and stay competitive.

An experienced consultant will have a well-structured methodology for driving the requirements gathering process. It is not enough to sit down with a process owner and say 'give me all of your requirements.' That approach only frustrates the business process owner and inevitably only captures regularly used processes. There have been projects in which a junior consultant was given the task of gathering all of the business requirements for the Business Blueprint and relied solely on this technique in addition to providing a questionnaire. Needless to say, they each resulted in poor parallel testing results. The reason being is that more often than not, the system ends up being designed to handle 20 percent of the employee population. The other 80 percent of the population has relatively simple, straightforward business processes and requirements. Often, a business process owner will assign a subject matter expert (SME) to work with the consultant. When asked general questions like "can you please provide me with all of your processes," the SME will typically respond with general processes that are used by the general population because working with the consultant is not the SME's primary purpose or job responsibility. They are busy performing their normal job duties. This is especially true in today's economy where productivity is essential to a company's survival. A good, experienced consultant knows that a company will have exceptions in the form of negotiated terms of hire (e.g. extra vacation), grandfathered policies, highly compensated employees, etc. that only apply to a small percentage of the employee population, and these situations will cause most of the exception configuration. This also happens to be one of the most visible areas in case because this group typically includes the stakeholders and champions of the project.

The experienced consultant will guide the SME through each area in a logical fashion to ensure effective and efficient use of the Subject Matter Expert's time. For instance, instead of just asking the SME to explain the company's time away policies, an experienced consultant will ask for the written policy that addresses the company's time away policy. The consultant will then consolidate the various types of leave, the amount, the eligibility criteria, etc. and then formulate any questions based on what's in the policy. The consultant will then proceed to inquire as to whether there are any exceptions to what has been communicated. Based on the reply, an experienced consultant knows what follow-on questions to ask in order to properly configure the system. This requires not only good communication and analytical skills but also the ability to translate those requirements mentally into a high-level system design. An example of this experience level is having the SME communicate that new hires with the company are allowed one week of vacation per calendar year unless they negotiate additional vacation as part of their hiring agreement. An experience consultant immediately thinks, "The system will need a date type on infotype 0041—Date Specifications to capture a date to perform a sonority calculation."

A vital step in constructing the Business Blueprint—but not part of the Blueprint deliverable—is ensuring that the consultant and the business process owner and/or SME understand each other. This may seem like an obvious no brainer but it has been the cause of a few implementation delays. The misunderstanding discussed here is not due to language barriers but rather business nomenclature. A company will have its own jargon, which is a combination of the industry it operates in along with its internal culture. In like manner, SAP has its own jargon as well. Case in point, a company communicated to its employees they will accrue two hours of sick leave every payroll period for a total sick leave entitlement of fifty-six hours per year (the company had a bi-weekly payroll which equated to twenty-six pay roll periods a year). The SME communicated to the consultant that the company had a policy that granted employees fifty-six hours of sick leave entitlement accrued two hours per payroll period. The consultant configured the system to satisfy the business requirement. The system worked just fine. However, it failed user acceptance testing...not because it wasn't calculating properly but because on SAP standard delivered quota report (both in the back-office and in Employee Self-Service (ESS)) had a field named "Entitlement." It was used to capture the year-to-date accrual balance for the quota. The employees and the HR staff knew that they receive fifty-six hours of sick leave entitlement per year and when they saw only two hours of entitlement, they thought the system was shorting them fifty-four hours. There was a significant level of effort put in to change management in order to communicate this to employees and get this cleared with the union population there, which caused a slight delay in the schedule.

Along the same vein is the topic of various concepts. Many companies struggle with the concept of Positive Time versus Negative Time (or Exception Time). Why use one over the other? Should employees record their time in clock-times or elapsed time? There are no hard and fast rules, but there are some general guidelines based on the desired downstream results and regulatory requirements. An experienced consultant is able to effectively communicate the differences and recommend a strategy based on the requirements. Another often-misunderstood concept is that of Salary Non-Exempt versus Hourly employees. This is a United States specific concept. The Non-Exempt status is referring to having to comply with FLSA laws. Many companies misclassify their employees. In addition, when these types of employees are assigned to a semi-monthly payroll period, they are sometimes incorrectly treated as hourly employees. Meanwhile, the consultant treats these employees like their name implies...Salary Non-Exempt. This results in the system producing calculations that are inconsistent with process owner expectations. To ensure a smooth implementation, the nomenclature and common concepts must be discussed so that both the company and the consultant are on the same page.

Once the Business Blueprint has been created and signed, it is time to move to the Realization phase of the implementation in which the system build takes place. This is where focus and interaction of the implementation team is more on the SAP system and each other and less on the business process owners and SMEs. At the core of this is the technical team that is responsible for setting up the SAP landscape, which includes the sandbox, development, quality assurance, production environments, or clients. This landscape, along with the transport strategy, then needs to be communicated to team members responsible for the configuration of the system. In addition, if the Employee Self-Service is to be used, the portal environments need to be set up to mirror the SAP landscape with a development, quality assurance, and production portal. Many incidents such as configuration in the wrong client, lost configuration, and overwritten configuration can be avoided by having a properly set up landscape and clearly communicated transport strategy.

There are several overarching factors that influence the approach that should be taken when performing Time Management system configuration. First, is the scope of the implementation global or just one country? If the scope is global, is there a country version available for one or more of the countries being implemented? Country versions are enhancements of the core SAP system. They provide country specific functionality to comply with regulatory laws. For instance, there are regulations in Poland that require special information for social insurance and leave quotas are based on the employee's entire working life, not just seniority at the current company. Custom infotypes, reports, and user exits would be needed in order to meet these requirements in the standard core SAP system. Installing the Poland country version provides the additional tables, reports, and functionality required to support Polish law. However, an experienced technical team would be needed to load the country version into the system along with a functional consultant who has experience with country versions because not all country versions play nicely with other country versions. Even after application of the country version, there is a need to further configure new tables and schema rules.

Second, are multiple consultants working on the Time Management configuration? If so, there should be a division of duties so that changes to a table or schema made by one consultant are not overridden by another consultant. There are other subtleties faced by multiple consultants that are not encountered by a sole consultant. For instance, table T503 is not country specific. Changes made to one country affect all other employee subgroup grouping settings. Even though a screen is presented with a drop down for the country, this only filters the view... it does not limit settings.

Lastly, is Concurrent Employment activated? If so, the standard Time Evaluation program, RPTIME00, cannot be used. Instead, the new program RPTIME01 must be used. If a consultant has no experience with Concurrent Employment, the entire implementation is jeopardy. This is due to the fact that a different master data database is used and functions within the schema operate differently. In a Concurrent Employment model, employees occupy multiple positions each with their own Personnel Number assignment.

Testing takes place towards the end of the Realization phase. However, before any tests (besides unit tests) are executed, a testing strategy and subsequent plan should be developed. These are needed to define what is going to be tested (e.g. overtime calculation, vacation accruals, etc.), what population is being tested (e.g. hourly employees, salary non-exempt employees working in California, etc.), what time period (e.g. a payroll period that incorporates holiday), expected results, exit criteria, who will conduct the testing, how will the data be set up, who will execute the tests, what environment will testing take place in, etc. Test case scenarios should be created based on the requirements captured in the Business Blueprint.

Finally, consideration should be given to change management as it relates to training the employee population. Even the design of the system is somewhat constrained by the employee population. While it would be nice to transition everyone in the company to Employee Self-Service on the portal, this is often not feasible for certain types of companies. For instance, some companies have packaging plants in Mexico that employ skilled labor. Many of those employees have never used a computer and don't have access to one either at home or on the shop floor. It's best to use time clocks and paper request forms for time off.

How does a company train a large geographically dispersed workforce to use Employee Self-Service? How does a company train its Time Administrators and Time Keepers to use the back-office? Solutions to these challenges depend on the resources of the company. Some companies have used webinars to conduct live trainings, some have used computer-based on demand training, and still others have used the train the trainer approach. Whatever the approach, the strategy and planning must begin in the middle of the Blueprinting process in order to ensure success.

Appendix A
Contributors' Background

Scott Burton
Whitaker-Taylor, Inc., Atlanta, GA

Scott Burton is the Managing Director of Whitaker-Taylor, an SAP consulting firm specializing in extended team services for production support and integration projects. In this role he helps clients maximize their investments in SAP software by streamlining their application support and enhancing the usability of their system through business process improvement and implementation services, which provide new and enhanced software functionality.

Scott has more than a decade of SAP HR consulting and application support experience. Scott has managed applications support operations for more than fifteen different global, national, and regional companies spanning industries such as manufacturing, automotive, retail, business services, and energy and gas.

The breadth of his experience enables him to fulfill multiple roles ranging from implementation consultant to support analyst to account manager to executive sponsor. Scott has presented at several SAP conferences on both technical SAP topics and on the support challenges SAP clients face with centralized support and with decentralized operations. In addition, Scott frequently conducts educational webinars and end-user training for Whitaker-Taylor clients and for the industry.

A native of White Plains, New York, Scott graduated from the University of Georgia with a B.S Degree in Management Information Systems. As an active member of his community, Scott has provided support for a number of charities through Whitaker-Taylor. Scott lives with his wife and two daughters in Atlanta, Georgia.

Steven Chihos

Steven J. Chihos, PMP, is an independent Organizational Change Leader with theBigRocks, LLC in Orlando, Florida. Over the course of his thirty-year career, Steven's roles have ranged from being a bit-twiddling techie to a people-focused facilitator, from being a loyal team member to acting as the ruthless project manager, from serving as an executive to mopping floors as the lowest guy on the org chart. For the past decade, he's guided individual leaders, teams, and organizations through the process of successfully implementing strategic change by diligently applying his methodology called "theBigRocks of Change." He also writes a popular blog for Change Agents at
http://theBigRocks.com.

Michael Feast

Michael Feast has over 12 years experience with consulting assignments involving all phases of SAP implementations. He has significant experience in the functional configuration of SAP Personnel Administration, Time Management, Employee Self-Service (ESS), SAP Workflow, Payroll, Cross Application Time Sheet (CATS), and Organization Management. Through his experiences, Michael has been able to amass a varied set of skills that bridge the gap between technology and business function including business process reengineering, business, and technical analysis.

Michael has designed and implemented SAP Human Capital Management (HCM) transformation solutions for clients in various industries including Public Sector, Pharmaceuticals, Oil and Gas, Manufacturing and Industrial. He has led diverse teams in designing business processes and implementing solutions in the various areas of SAP HCM including Time and Payroll.

Michael has a Masters of Science degree in Information Systems and Decision Sciences with a minor in Internal Auditing from Louisiana State University. He continues to assist companies in the successful implementation of their SAP HCM systems.

Tracey Groomes

Tracey Groomes graduated with a MBA (Masters of Business Administration) from Rutgers University and is the CEO of Brit Incorporated. Her role includes a practicing SAP Human Capital Consultant with a specification in functional technical Enterprise Learning. Brit Incorporated focuses on global manufacturing, service, and human resource entities in the Private and Public Sectors. Brit Incorporated is a United States-based company headquartered in Texas.

Tracey has over twenty years of operations experience and more than ten years of experience providing consulting services. Her expertise lies with her ability to direct and utilize systems to promote efficiency, documentation, and compliance in public and private administrative and operational environments.

Raaz Karimi

Raaz Karimi was born in 1966 in Bombay, India. Raaz moved to the United States after completing high school and studied at the University of Texas at Austin and got his degree in Management Information Systems.

Raaz's professional career began as a programmer at J.C Penney. After five years Raaz decided to become an independent consultant. With a focus in Human Capital Management, Raaz started working with SAP during the summer of 1997 with a focus on Human Capital Management module. Over the past 14 years Raaz has taken on various roles that range from programmer, development team lead, and consulting manager. Raaz feels fortunate to have had the opportunity to work within the private, public, and federal sectors, as well as on an onshore-offshore model.

When Raaz is not working for SAP clients he enjoys golf and tennis.

Saaz Karimi

Saaz was born in India and moved to the United States during High School. He moved to Dallas upon graduation to attend University of North Texas (Denton).

He postponed graduation from college due to health/medical issues. Events that occurred were life changing but also a process in learning to overcome the greatest challenge one can face.

He graduated college with a degree in business management with a focus on hospitality management. Upon graduation, he worked on onsite/offshore projects for a small multimedia company. He worked as a manager/go-between for the customer and offshore developers. His IT network led to meeting SAP consultants and sparked an interest to learn the software implementation side of SAP HR. He went back to college to pursue Information Technology courses as part of a Masters Program at University of Texas Dallas. He had a chance to start learning SAP HR from his brother who is an SAP technical consultant and project manager for 10+ years now, and that lead to an opportunity to work for SAP America.

He worked for SAP America as an SAP HCM functional consultant within the Org Management, Personnel Administration, and e Recruiting modules. He worked on full life cycle implementations of HR and one of the largest ever e-recruiting projects. While working for SAP America, he had the opportunity to work with several Platinum Level consultants and learned tools and methodologies that make for successful implementations. He is currently working as an independent SAP HCM consultant with a focus on new HR implementations, upgrades, and keeping current with the latest SAP releases.

Sean Mallon

Sean Mallon is the co-founder and managing partner of HodgePodge Solutions, a wholesale aggregator of *SAP Partner* and third party software and hardware. In addition, he works as an SAP HCM Consultant with a focus on designing and delivering the Personnel Administration, Benefits, and Enterprise Compensation Management modules

with integration to Payroll. His passion is following and studying trends in the information technology market with a dream of building the first "true" e-Procurement hub for ERP Partner products (i.e. certified and non-certified)—an on-line setting where a client can peruse and purchase software in bundles while saving money and receiving expert service from its vendors. For further information on this groundbreaking concept, please contact Sean at
sean.mallon@hodgepodgehub.com.

Jan Redmond

Growing up in Kansas City, Missouri afforded Jan a very diverse background. Jan has been able to leverage an awesome education, which included Immanuel Lutheran School and William Jewell College. Jan's mother, Jacqueline, only achieved a tenth grade education (later got her GED), but she constantly endorsed getting a college degree at the very least. Jan gives major kudos to his mother for her support and love.

Jan has been grounded in athletics, specifically football, since the third grade. Jan doesn't know whether it was becoming a collegiate All American, playing in Europe, or recent induction to his alma mater's Football Hall of Fame that best defines his football memories/accolades. Jan has spent eleven years coaching little league or Pop Warner football in North Texas watching young men mature within the confines of football.

Jan's professional SAP experience involves an array of roles within major corporations. Jan's experience as a Facilities Management supervisor at Xerox and an Executive HCM Solutions Engineer at SAP has given him priceless exposure to industries and companies globally.

Jan's family defines him. The unwavering support of his wife, Pamela, for twenty-three-plus years has really provided his foundation. Pamela is an exceptional wife, friend, and soul mate. Her support and her passion for their family are paramount. Jan's true legacy is his children (his two sons Rinaldo and Avery).

Currently, Jan is the National SAP HCM Support lead at Capgemini. Jan pretty much evangelizes SAP HCM and Capgemini's SAP practice to organizations nationally. Jan has been at Capgemini for nearly two years.

Jan's chapter was inspired from his vast experiences around software sales for nearly twenty years. Jan's previous employment at Xerox, Ceridian, Oracle, SAP, and now Capgemini all have provided him exceptional insight into what have been some pitfalls and best practices while attempting to reach nirvana from diminutive and colossal software purchases.

Maxine Wood

Maxine Wood is a certified SAP HR Consultant who has specialized in Benefits for thirteen years.

She has a Bachelor's Degree (B.S. Business Administration/Marketing from the State University of New York-Oswego, 1994). She was hired by Deloitte Consulting in 1996 as an Educational Services Consultant. She translated functional SAP information into training documentation, which allowed her to understand how the entire system is integrated.

She became certified by SAP in 1998. She's been an Independent Consultant under her own company since 2001. Her expertise and interest is with the Benefits module and its integration with Personnel Administration and Payroll. She has worked with various sized organizations and performed numerous project activities. Among her favorites are configuration and writing functional specifications for custom development pertaining to Benefits.

She is categorized as a Business Analyst, Functional Consultant or Subject Matter Expert. She works hard and welcomes new challenges with each assignment.

She is currently working on a Public Sector engagement with Concurrent Employment.

Editor

About the Editor

LaShonda Rahming has provided consulting services for many of the world's most admired brands. She has been named as an emerging leader in the December issue of *Inc. Magazine* in 2010 and is a bestselling author. She is a speaker, a vocalist, and a consultant with more than thirteen years of experience. LaShonda's passion for innovative consulting has catapulted her to a national platform as a leader in collaboration. LaShonda left her role as Partner to pursue consultative innovation in 2008 and is now the Chief Collaboration Officer of ALL About Collaboration. Her experience building high-achieving teams, implementing successful processes, and guiding implementations for top-tier companies has provided the backbone of ALL About Collaboration. Offering a rare blend of sales experience and Big ERP consulting experience, her creative and operational strengths have allowed LaShonda to achieve uncommon results for some of the country's largest and most complex organizations. An accomplished Partner, Director, Consultant, Project Manager and Business Process Strategist, her vision and expertise has driven many organizations to increased sales and streamlined approaches.

The collaboration model that LaShonda has come up with is truly relevant as she is taking social networking to another level and inviting others to use the ALL About Collaboration platform to get honest responses and a competitive advantage. Ms. Rahming is known for her dynamic team leadership and her ability to implement cutting edge solutions. Learn more about her platform for collaboration at http://www.allaboutcollaboration.com.

Books

Other Happy About® Books

Purchase these books at Happy About http://happyabout.com or at other online and physical bookstores.

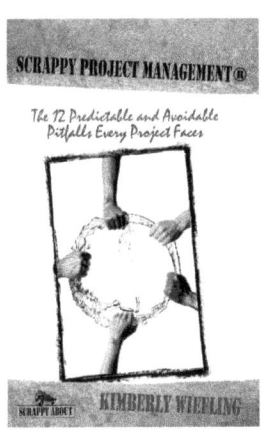

Scrappy Project Management

This book is for people who need to get things done...especially project managers

Paperback $19.95
eBook $14.95

42 Rules of Employee Engagement

This book is loaded with practical advice and actions you can take away to begin building an engaged team.

Paperback $19.95
eBook $14.95

**#BUSINESS SAVVY PM
tweet Book01**

In this book you will perceive the path to understanding the business value of a project—and why your company is undertaking it.

Paperback $19.95
eBook $14.95

**#RISK MANAGEMENT
tweet Book01**

This handy title is meant to be an introduction or a refresher on how to determine risk and practice risk management in your everyday work habits.

Paperback $19.95
eBook $14.95

www.ingramcontent.com/pod-product-compliance
Ingram Content Group UK Ltd.
Pitfield, Milton Keynes, MK11 3LW, UK
UKHW021303180426
11947UKWH00015B/998